Each human being is unique,
unprecedented, unrepeatable.

Rene Dubos
So Human an Animal, 1968

The Art of the Very Young:

CHARLES E. MERRILL PUBLISHING COMPANY
A Bell & Howell Company
Columbus, Ohio 43216

An Indicator of Individuality

A Multimedia Program

BETTY LARK-HOROVITZ

To my children and grandchildren
who from infancy made me aware
of the diversity and force of personality

Published by
Charles E. Merrill Publishing Company
A Bell & Howell Company
Columbus, Ohio 43216

This book was set in Trade Gothic and Kabel Light.
Editing and production by Julie Estadt.
Cover and album design by Will Chenoweth.

Library of Congress Catalog Card Number: 76-5958

International Standard Book Number: 0-675-08571-3

1 2 3 4 5 6 7 8 9 10 / 80 79 78 77 76

Printed in the United States of America

Preface

The basis of this program is a longitudinal study of the art output of thirty very young children, some from their very first scribble. This unusually large compilation reflects the view of the author that no amount of description can replace the necessity to "see," and this MEDIAPAK audiovisual program is enriched by hundreds of pictures in color and black and white. The coordinated use of text and MEDIAPAK components provides comprehensive and informative coverage of the entire field of the very young child's development in art activities.

Emphasis is placed on understanding the importance of the child's early art activity as an individual expression and way of learning. While the core of the program is the children's illustrations themselves, its uniqueness is in the individuality, the spontaneity, and the developmental cues offered by these illustrations. The pictures are documented by age, sex, media, and titles (frequently provided by the child), and often annotated by comments made by parents or child at the time the work was done.

Picture biographies of four individual children are the outcome of the exceptional opportunity to observe their spontaneous art activities from earliest childhood into the beginning of elementary school. The art included in their biographies was selected from an impressive output.

Throughout the text, "she" has been used for teacher and "he" for child merely for simplification. This indicates no bias for either teachers' or children's sex.

Acknowledgments

The author wishes to express her gratitude to many. First and most of all, Dorothy Bennett helped on this program with the greatest understanding, support, and encouragement through the years of assembling, compiling, and writing. Rosamund D. Gardner, Ph.D., Chief Psychologist of the Child Development Center of Children's Hospital Medical Center, Oakland, California, contributed the comprehensive Introduction, a psychological foundation based on valuable new concepts.

The parents, especially the mothers, of the thirty children in this study consented to the use of and cooperated by keeping all of their children's work and comments, added their own observations, and answered and raised questions.

Catherine Landreth, Professor Emeritus of child psychology and author of books and articles on child development; Edith Newton, biochemist by profession and informed layman in child education; and Fannie Oltman, teacher in private schools and interested observer of child art, read the manuscript, discussed it, and offered their points of view.

Elinor Griffin of the Griffin Nursery School in Berkeley, California, who is particularly concerned with and interested in art activities of preschoolers, and Diane Meyer, formerly of the International Child Art Center in San Francisco, now conducting her own art school, the San Francisco Children's Art Center, were helpful in their discussions on teaching art to the very young.

Thanks is also given to Robert G. Norton, Bob Hedges, and the staff of the photo laboratory of the Berkeley Commercial Photo Co., Berkeley, California. They helped patiently to rescue many reproductions of drawings for which children used color nearly identical with the color of their paper or that were done on waste paper, many times folded, or that the children themselves had crumpled up when finished. Thanks is also given for the understanding help of the Berkeley Blue Print Company.

How to Use This Program

This program consists of a text and accompanying MEDIAPAK audio and visual components intended for integrated use. Though the program is flexible and may be used by both individuals and groups, a structure for using the material has been incorporated.

Begin by reading Part One of the text and continue with Part Two, Module One, until the first reference to MEDIAPAK 1 is reached (page 26). View and listen to the specified frames in the audiovisual presentation, at the end of which you will be directed back to the text. Continue following the program as directed in the text and tape narration.

Integration is complete between text and *related* MEDIAPAK components. However, not all text modules have related media, and no specific instruction is given as to when to read these or when to begin reading each new text module. These reading assignments will be made by your instructor, or you may simply follow the sequence of the text itself at your own pace. The relationship between text and media is shown in the Contents, page viii.

The tape contains an inaudible pulse that changes visual frames on automatic equipment, and an audible tone indicates when to change frames manually if you are using nonautomated equipment. Whatever type of equipment you are using, remember that you can stop the AV equipment at any time should you wish to study individual frames for longer than the time allowed.

Contents

Part One

Introduction

Overview

The author of *The Art of the Very Young* hopes that this audiovisual program may open a new awareness of the value of spontaneous art activity for very young children. Perhaps it will also challenge adults to make a greater effort to understand the importance of this special kind of activity From infancy to school age, "art" is a child's important way of exploring his own feelings, clarifying his own problems, and developing a way of communication about his relations to his environment and the people of his world.

It is important that a child's art be seen as his own individual expression — not to be stereotyped into a framework, not to be compared with adult art, not to be seen in competition with his own or another child's performance.

Children's creations seldom produce "Art," but instead offer a revealing and different perspective of what the child thinks and feels about his world and his place in it.

A child's first marks with a stick in the dirt, with fingers on the wall, or with a pencil on paper are less attempts at art than sheer joy in movement and expression. Just as a young child needs to run, to play, to laugh, he needs opportunity to freely scribble, paint, and model. These are efforts of body and mind necessary to his growth.

His early creations may appear to be meaningless scribbles, but they may be the child's best way to express feelings he cannot yet put into words. Child art, whatever its degree of accomplishment, has unadulterated sincerity. It is an avowal of the child's experienced sensations, feelings, and perceptions. It gives evidence of his developing personality, his striving to be part of his experience in his expanding environment.

To the Reader

Each child sees a different world because each child is different. His interests, aims, opinions and problems are different from those of other children, even his brothers and sisters. His drawings and comments mirror himself in his own individual world.

A conviction that continuing study should be made of the art activities of very young children led the author to follow closely the spontaneous art of thirty young children whose early work had come to her attention. Through the generous cooperation of their parents, it has been possible to assemble and study their art productions, some from the very earliest beginnings, some through non-interrupted or seldom interrupted activity over a period of months or years. This longitudinal study material is useful because it permits appraisal not only of the variety and meaningful development of individual art expression, but also because it permits insight into changes of attitude as well as development and continuation of certain personality traits. It also is significant in its confirmation of the observable fact that, despite individual differences, children the world over have similar ways of self-exploration through art expression. Here is evidence, once more, of the universality of children's need to express themselves and the startling yet varied similarities in the way they do it—if left to themselves.

This program is based on a prolonged study of drawings and paintings of thirty children, but the conclusions stem in part from the author's more than forty years' observation of children's art activities in homes, schools, and museums as well as from a large personal collection of examples of children's work from one and one-half to eighteen years of age in the United States and in Europe. In the course of teaching art to children of nearly all ages and of experimental studies of the art abilities of eleven hundred children, the author was astounded to find enough pronouncedly different individual pictorial expression to enable her to recognize the work of a considerable number of children without knowing them personally.

The strong individual character of the work of so many children was not only surprising, but seemed to offer ample evidence that differences within the similarities in children's art achievement would be of unsuspected value in revealing differences in general personality development as well. Furthermore, this pointed in a direction not central to most previous research. Most early studies had as their goal the finding of common denominators in pictorial characteristics of children at given ages or developmental levels in drawing. They were designed to gain information regarding the "average" child, and were based on the widely-held concept of children's art efforts as beginning steps in a progression toward adult art. This view is no longer held. Child art is a kind of art in itself and should be valued as such and so judged.

Alschuler and Hattwick's valuable pioneer study was based essentially on the easel paintings of very young children. Although aware of the home art activities of these children, the researchers based their study on nursery school performances. It pointed to the great importance of art work to the growth of the normal child, yet seemed clinical in approach, behavior-oriented, and gave the impression of art activity as a therapy. The re-publication of Alschuler and Hattwick's work points to the increasing interest in art activities of very young children. It demonstrates, too, that young children are much influenced by school surroundings in the nature of their art productions. However, some biographical studies of the past, pointing up the young child's art activity, support the differences between children's self-initiated art work at home and that done in school. There are all too few examples of continuous observation over a period of years of uninhibited, "spur-of-the-moment" art work of individual children of very young age. The numerous studies on child art deal with only one example or relatively few works produced by large numbers of different children, usually of school age, and based on situations initiated in school.

This program offers continuing study of periods in the spontaneous art activities of thirty widely-separated children. Its focus is intimate analyses of these collections, so astonishing in their diversity, and particularly of four children's developments that are descriptive of the separate directions the very young may follow. Background material for understanding the fragments of "art biographies" here given is provided for the reader in a careful presentation of the psychological development of the very young child by child psychologist Rosamund D. Gardner who discusses the issues of present-day theories of child development and the stages of mental and social growth in these early years.

Anyone interested in young children will find that the observations made in this study offer ways to look at the art of the very young and to see in it useful clues to their developing personalities. In their picturing activities, *children explain to themselves the outer world as it is reflected in them and assimilated by them,* a free coming-to-terms with the living and mechanized world before they are "taught" how to do it. Though there are other ways of expression and though not every child takes to picture-making, this is a particularly useful and fundamental basis of growth and understanding for them. It is not meaningless play but *a way of learning* developed by them. It is work; it is self-instruction and clarification.

Psychologist Jerome Singer says that children have two kinds of mental recording systems—one based on words, the other on imagery. Once a vocabulary is acquired, the verbal system is quick and efficient, but the memory bank of images is very important for storing details and understanding information related to complex concepts. Therefore, the young child who has been encouraged to explore through art activity may well be better equipped to learn.

From its combination of actual life situations, this program offers teachers and parents the tools for a more intimate understanding of this important developmental activity and guidance in how to observe and encourage children to pursue, enjoy, and benefit from individual, spontaneous art experience.

Introduction

Some Aspects of the Psychological

Many factors affect a child's growth and learning, and these factors act one upon the other in a complex network of relationships.

From the first formative months, children undergo a series of normal, age-related changes in growth and maturity. Their physical functioning as well as their minds operate at each stage within the general limits of a genetically given constitution and a level of maturation. Size and strength determine much of their physical performance. The degree of differentiation and interpretation in psychological processes—memory, perception, language, and reasoning—determine their adaptation to people and the material environment. The behavior that emerges by ordered sequence from stage to stage reflects a child's growing potential for social learning, competence, maturity, and skill.

A further factor in relation to unique constitution and special abilities in differing stages is clearly the manner in which children can both modify and be influenced by their environment. The child's experiences in the family, school, and the external world influence all aspects of the developing self. The environment may help to accelerate or enhance or may delay or distort the patterns of growing maturity. It will inevitably confer a special quality on enduring achievements, personality, and life style.

The child's constitution, his maturation level, and his experience are closely interwoven; therefore, one should proceed cautiously in applying an oversimplified theory of child development to the study of children's problems. In setting up teaching or remedial procedures, however, a widely based theory of normal development gives strength and focus to the study of variations from the normal, provided individual differences are also well understood. For example, one can apply knowledge of the

Development of the Young Child

ROSAMUND D. GARDNER

unfolding sequences of eye-hand skills in normal infants as a standard by which to assess achievement level in any infant with special problems. The life experiences that naturally shape these developmental sequences in normal infants enable us to see what must be supplemented in the environment of the handicapped infant. To overcome the handicap and assure optimal development, however, calls for a sensitive blending of prescribed curriculum with the unique features of each child. Herein lies the art of adapting and applying theoretical knowledge to meet a practical challenge in working with children.

Theories of child development have in common a general concern with identifying and accounting for the changing levels of the child's behavior as he progresses from stage to stage. Though there are discernable unities within stages, wide individual differences occur between children in the quality, duration, and contents of stage-specific behavior.

The child's behavior within a stage may be highly influenced by the nature of what he sets out to do. There may be sex differences or differences due to previous experiences that affect the child's readiness to perform. In short, individual differences overwhelm an observer, as they do parent and teacher. In order to fully understand the child, the teacher learns to observe closely over a period of months, the parent over a span of years. *Intensive study of individuals over an extended time may yield more than the collective generalization. Indeed, many insights on child development have been achieved in this way.* A longitudinal study like the research on which *The Art of the Very Young* is based is rare and can reveal quality of growth through change that short-term statistical studies cannot uncover.

Writers who have built their theories on longitudinal observations and clinical experience include Arnold Gesell in the field of motor development; Sigmund Freud whose concern was primarily in psycho-social adjustment throughout the life cycle; and Jean Piaget whose research and theory has given a major spurt to the study of mental development from infancy to adolescence.

Gesell's position leans heavily toward a primary theory of maturation in which the following elements are included. As the child's body grows, his physical ability differentiates in an ordered cephalo-to-caudal sequence. *Maturation of function precedes use.* The child cannot perform until he has achieved a *state of readiness.* The ceiling placed upon his performance is minimally affected by learning, though he requires a facilitation in the environment to exercise a matured function.

Freud's work—he is often referred to as the great pessimist on human behavior—is difficult to sum up briefly. Perhaps his reputation in the area of child development has been gained largely by emphasis on his *stage-related theory of the psycho-sexual development of the very young child.* What has become clear, in retrospect, is that this was primarily a theory of neurosis, arrived at by the study of mentally ill adults and children. However, from the work in psycho-pathology we can now salvage many benign and important themes in the life of the normal child upon which Freud threw much light: instinctual behavior in infancy supporting the new science of ethology; the basic drives and patterns of energy discharge; cultural attitudes around sex-typing by parents and society; the development of *competence and self-esteem*—loosely referred to as *ego-psychology*—and so on. These are but a small sample of the ongoing work in child psychology, psychiatry, and education owing its inspiration and inception to the work of Freud.

What of Piaget? Much of his work, being current, suffers both from overhasty and superficial evaluation and application—some remains untranslated. English speaking workers in the field are sometimes left unaware of the full scope and implication of the steady flow of work maintained at Piaget's Geneva Institute. He and his collaborator, Bärbel Inhelder, have clearly described scientifically intriguing experiments utilizing the materials and experience of the child's day-to-day life. They have shown vastly creative planning and clinical expertise with children in revealing what it is like to be in a child's world. Piaget has evolved a systemization of the *stages of intellectual development in childhood:* Sensory-motor intelligence from birth–18 months or 2 years; Pre-logical thinking, 2–7 years; Concrete operational (logical) thinking, 7–12 years; Formal logical thinking from 12 to adulthood. Some psychologists question the full validity of this theoretical model because of the complexity of the issues with which it deals. In any view, Piaget's work remains instrumental in giving theoretical coherence to many formerly puzzling and challenging aspects of child development.

In the perspective of the child's behavior, what is it that one needs to know about children? How do children learn? What guidelines must one possess in observing and drawing conclusions?

At any given stage, a child's behavior is largely concerned with obtaining meaning and relevance, establishing habits and certainties, and classifying and storing knowledge. Therefore his functioning can be interpreted along these lines.

Like the scientist, he must develop hypotheses that he must test and confirm or discard. Like the artist, he must follow the urge to concretize the significant emotion or thought taking shape within him.

In order to observe and understand the development of the child, one must discern the meaningful elements that comprise his behavior. One must understand: *why* he sharpens his observation and perception; *why* he is absorbed in the constructions put forth and shaped by his mind; *how* he deals with implacable evidence of his senses; *how* he deals with the ephemeral image and the insatiable wish.

Some answers to these questions come by seeing the child as an experimenter, creating and improvising under the pressure of partial knowledge and understanding. *The primary objective of the young child's activities is self-enhancement—whether in self-expression or in response to constraints imposed by the environment.*

THE EMERGENCE OF THE SENSE OF SELF

A most vital issue in the early development of the child is the provision afforded by his material environment and his social contacts for the experiences and maturation of his sense of being a person. As childhood progresses, he builds the foundation for three aspects of his knowledge of self.

First, he has a bodily "me," derived directly from action, employing muscles and movement skills. He also experiences tension and release in bodily functions and can absorb from the world of sights, sounds, tastes, and textures sensual experience to sustain the active functioning of his senses.

Second, a personal "me" is evolved from the contact with people and the interaction with objects. The child comes into possession of his world and begins to know himself as an effective element in changing it and having power over it. He can regulate the impinging events to obtain what he wishes and needs from them.

Third, a social "me" arises when his childlike egocentricity gives place to a more inclusive and understanding social awareness. As he begins to orient himself within a new, more clearly-defined psychological boundary of self, he can begin to take into account differing viewpoints between himself and the other. To review this concept developmentally it will be useful to trace briefly the interaction of these main themes from infancy through childhood.

Wide horizons open up from early life for the development of individuality. As infants, children experience, with rich spontaneity, the life of the moment. Their rudimentary powers of thought, reflection, and reason are tied to the development of sensory awareness and physical movement.

Infants reach, grasp, let go, touch, and suck. They avidly explore with eye, ear, mouth, and fingers. Their attention springs into being with the interplay of voice, with exchanges in smiling, or with the renewal of body contacts when they are lifted, held, or fed. They yield to physical support, react to discomfort, and express states of inner need and pleasure by fretting or cooing. At times, they may be quietly receptive but they also balance this passivity with the play of their strong, lively impulses. They command attention, extend their mental world by explorative efforts. They "happen on" new experience to which they react like an inventor or a person bent on acquiring new skills.

With this repertoire, they can establish, from the start, links between experience and action. Their sense of self is thus rooted in their sensory awareness, active involvement, and deep sensuality. Something further, however, must accompany this wide range of sensory-motor experiences. For infants to fully identify themselves within their own acts and feelings, they need affirmation from a person who is a shared part of the exchanges and who helps to bring about their transactions with outer experience.

The milieu of the awakening of the infant's personal "me" is fostered by the good mother or mother surrogate.* Many fluid empathic exchanges occur in the course of her innumerable caretaking acts. She and the infant exchange smiles, playful gestures, and expressive "talk" in which the infant sees glimpses of himself reflected from the mother as if in a mirror. His perception reinforces his imitation. In this learning process he can transform images and actions into inner states of self-awareness.

The normal good mother helps to maintain this awakening sense of personal self by some important and natural attitudes implicit and embodied in her moment-to-moment and day-to-day care of her child. She seeks his cooperation by synchronizing her rhythms to his. She shapes his behavior and modifies her own to achieve a mutual harmony. She gives him opportunity to anticipate her movements and approach. She gathers him up and carries him so that his body is securely and comfortably positioned in her arms. In each single purpose as she goes about her many care-taking acts for him the infant can begin to recognize and associate meaning with her actions because they are visibly understood.

If the creation of a sense of self-hood occurs, In Winnicott's phrase (Winnicott, 1965), within "the holding actions" of the mother, here then is a link between mothering and the expansion of the self in self-

*Today some fathers take on this role and what follows about "mothering" could be said of "fathering" when the father's focus is as intense and practical in day-to-day care of the child as the traditional mother's.

expression. Perhaps the sense of self is the vital element giving form and vigor to original and spontaneous child art. Moreover, it follows that the child must feel at home, "held" in the protective intimacy of a personal relationship, actual or internalized, before he can give himself freely to drawing, painting, and creative play.

The sense of a personal "me" continues to emerge and develop new aspects in the second stage of childhood. As the child gains mobility and physical independence, the life sphere alters radically. Instead of being held or supported, feeling the strength of his body in cooperation with his mother, he is now able to obey every restless impulse with independent freedom of action. His wishes soon begin to center on the issues of physical control and physical skill. The child begins to develop an ego, centered outwardly on the "wish to possess" and the "will to dominate." Underlying both is the deeper and stronger ego derived from the intrinsic satisfaction of competence and newly-found autonomy.

Paradoxically, as the two- to three-year-old child becomes capable of physical independence, he is also susceptible to fear and frustration. There is therefore a duality in his emotional life, which is a potential cause of great personal strain for the child unless good experiences have been stored up from babyhood. If he has experienced as an infant a secure relationship of love and care, this security bestows now a sense of trust. If the toddler and the three-year-old know that there will be support when they may need it, they will optimistically seek adventure in the world. They will also defy or test the prohibition of the person whose love and help they take for granted.

The ego, that aspect of self of which we are now speaking, thrives on experiences that give expression to and satisfy more than instinctual bodily needs. New patterns of association within perception and cognition begin to underly the child's interests and actions. It is now that drawings evolve from messing and scribbling and the child begins to imagine or intuit many things in the circles and lines he has made. He will "assimilate"—make what he has just put on the paper meaningful to himself—and ignore standards of accuracy and completeness. Thus, children begin to associate and even identify with the imaginative world that they are able to create by the new magic of their own imagery and ideas. Their artwork gives expression to new experiences of feeling and thinking. The ego, or the new personal self, is a conscious guide, drawing together in the work elements of inner and outer worlds.

What are the hazards in the growth of a good self-image at this stage? They seem to be twofold. There is, on the one hand, the battle of the child against the parent for the exercise of autonomy (Erikson, 1968). On the other hand, the child must come to terms with contradictory feelings within himself. Of particular interest is the Freudian viewpoint concerning the role played at this stage by mother and child in the bowel training process. Erikson writes this about the child: "The anal zone lends itself more than any other to the expression of stubborn insistence on conflicting impulses because . . . the [anal zone] is the modal zone for two contradictory modes which must become alternating, namely, retention and elimination (Erikson, 1968, p. 108)."

The child's "conflicting impulses" pose a severe test for any mutual regulation of bodily needs and the experience of love begun in infancy between mother and child. The child has to learn to "hold in" and to "give up" and in so doing loses some of the old spontaneity and dependency upon the mother. Bowel training in our culture is a strictly moral and utilitarian training, inaugurating by the mother a new standard of self-discipline and independence in the life of the child. When the training is carried through with harshness or rigidity or lack of warmth, the child rebels, gaining thereby a pseudo autonomy. This rebellion has a double edge since, in fact, the child wants his mother's care and protection to allay fears of danger and destruction that, though they emanate from fantasy, give the child great anxiety. The conflict created in the child is a battle between the forces within the ego that lead towards mature functioning and the falling back regressively on dependency needs associated with babyhood.

The self-image resulting from the personality conflict is expressed in the child's ambivalent forms of behavior. He seeks closeness but also violently rejects it—he hoards and clings to objects but then carelessly throws them away regardless of their former value to him. He can become destructive and cruel or he can show concern and even "love." If during this time the mother exercises moderation in her training demands and the child's impulse controls come by free will, some of the self-doubts and contradictory wishes will be resolved. The autonomy that then emerges is genuine. His balanced or adaptive self-control has been gained without loss of self-esteem. Self-doubt has been replaced with healthy self-assurance. When the child goes through this stage without severe disruption of close mother ties, his earlier bodily "me" is preserved within a new sense of a personal self—an ego identity based on autonomy and competence.

The third period in this sequence is concerned mainly with the development of a social self. The young child, in the preschool years, knows how to gain and keep attention, how to assert his will, how to ask questions, and how to invite help. He can also articulate wishes and feelings. However, in all these modes of behavior his orientation is mentally "centered" on personal issues. The term used by Piaget to denote this is "egocentric." This refers to a level of cognition and not to egotism or selfishness. The preschool child is unable to distinguish his own viewpoint from that of others, and cannot construct true three-dimensional notions of space. For example, when looking at pictures of mountains or houses taken from different sides, the child thinks that *all* views will look like the one view he perceives from where he stands. By the time the child reaches seven years, however, he can begin to make a mental reconstruction of where the photographer would have to stand to take the different views (Piaget, 1948). Until a child has achieved this important development in thought, he cannot compose pictures where size and distance are truly represented.

In a manner analogous with cognitive "decentering" in space, the preschool child begins slowly to recognize that the actions of others are promoted by wishes and intentions separate from his own. Following this, he becomes aware that relationships exist between other people and even though he is physically present to witness the interactions, he is nevertheless an "outsider." He thus becomes more certain about the distinctions between his own viewpoint and intent and the sphere of others. Also, he is able to grasp inter-subjective states existing in spheres of social interaction quite separate from his own.

This change in social awareness spurs the child on to communicate and cooperate and engenders his first genuine sympathy and altruistic feelings. In addition, because some of the limitations of cognitive egocentricity wane, children in the first school years can listen to others speaking and can make a mental reproduction of what is said without too much assimilative distortion*. They also can alter their own communication to gain the understanding of the person with whom they are speaking—a process highly interrelated with new language proficiency.

In these wider areas of social participation, the child begins to place different feeling values upon action. Interests, pleasures, and problems —always the regulators of action—begin to correspond with the new more social techniques and skills instead of being related to practical or two-person issues. Children from about seven years onward play games with rules, and they are able to see that scientific causes operate in natural events. Cognitive growth is always one side of the coin of the social self; growth in feeling values is the other.

How are the child's developing social interests and his new cognitive powers apparent in the relationship with parents? Several factors stand out for comment.

First, parents are figures whose power and authority have been a source of emotional ambivalence, especially in the years when the child first discovers his autonomy. Now a new compliance emerges and parents are promoted to positions of importance in the child's eyes since they represent some of the social values and expert social skills that are to be imitated.

Adaptation of this kind, through social imitation and identification, sometimes may present a problem. Much depends on the strength of the child's personal identity as to whether the social learning that takes place in the child constitutes true maturity. From affectionate, sensitive, and sup-

*See Piaget & Inhelder, 1969.

portive parents the child internalizes values and obligations that do not strain his yet childlike ego. If imitation of social norms is shallow and mechanical, on the other hand, ego weakness results. Winnicott describes this child as having "a sense of frame without a picture, a sense of form without retention of spontaneity (Winnicott, 1965, p. 158)." The group pressures that mount in intensity for this child may develop in him an attitude masquerading as prosocial. He may acquire a narrowness and intolerance that may result, over time, in an attitude incompatible with the general ideals of society.

A second factor in the child's social growth at this stage concerns his affectionate ties and his need for a special relationship with the parent—particularly the parent of the opposite sex. Traditionally, this stage is seen as a time when the child's intense emotional attachment is threatened by his growing awareness that the parent to whom he extends a special love is already engaged in another special relationship that excludes him. Whether or not this has overtones of the Freudian Oedipal complex, it is certainly the period when heterosexual affection slowly switches away from parents to peers. A large part of emotional energy is also re-engaged in creative work and play. Children at this stage become busy with skills, imaginative productions, competitive games, and like-sex companionship and interests.

Aiding and enriching the above processes of emotional-social growth is children's contact with traditional children's stories. At this stage they can glean from fairy tales the sense of human "goodness" or "badness"—seeing how fidelity and love bring happiness "ever after" or noting the downfall that follows acts of meanness or aggression.

THE DEVELOPMENT OF CONCEPTS AND THE EARLY GROWTH OF LANGUAGE

We can understand the development of mental processes in young children more fully if we break down the complex structure of human thinking into some of the elements of which it is composed. Piaget has helped us to see developmental significance and progression in children's thought.

Length

Here are some simple questions with which Piaget's research has been concerned. Why is it that young children cannot understand the applied usefulness of a ruler for measuring length? They seem to lack any implicit knowledge or standard measure. They improvise within constructions with approximate, intuitive guessing. If, for example, a child wishes to make a doll's shirt, the length may be guaged more or less correctly, but an estimate of the two-dimensional roundness of the body, in order to arrive at a suitable width, is very difficult.

We can guess at the difficulty if we see what children do if they are asked to compare the length of two lines placed one above the other when one line is curvilinear and the other straight but both begin and end at the same place. They judge the lines to be equal, not taking into account that there are curves in the one line and no curves in the other. If the curved line is replaced by a bent string and children are told to stretch out the string, they will see that it is longer than the straight line. However, on pushing it back again into curves to occupy the first position, they will say, as they said at first, that the string is the same length as the line above.

How is it that a child cannot use the new evidence to refute this faulty judgment? Again we see the problem in another simple experiment. When preschool children are asked to compare two sticks of equal lengths, placed one beneath the other, they note that they are equal if they are in alignment. If the same two sticks are placed out of alignment, one further forward than the other, they will say without hesitation that one stick is longer than the other. Apparently they remain unaware of the self-contradiction. Piaget's explanation here is that in the child of approximately three to six years, perception dominates over logic. Perceptually compelling aspects of a visual pattern bias the child's thought so that he cannot use the true logic that an older child can abstract from experience.

Space

How do young children come to know the properties of objects and their relationship in space? From babyhood on, a child's thought is shaped by the observation of physical change in objects as they move or as he handles them in increasingly skillful ways. In watching or touching an object, its differing angles present to his senses changing perceptual impressions. In this way, long before children can reason logically they come to recognize many of the properties of objects. This familiarity and practical knowledge applies also to their physical use of space. In both cases, however, they lack the conceptual power that lends to objects and physical space an enduring identity and formal completeness.

A seated infant of about six months old shows marked surprise when a toy or spoon drops from the table and he is able to locate it in its new place on the floor. At about eight months, however, when he can crawl, his surprise has gone and he can both locate and retrieve a castaway object. He goes after it with the zest and delight that often accompanies confidence in a new skill. His manner implies that he has acquired both a sense of the stable identity of an object wherever it moves in space and the means for locating it accurately.

This retrieval skill is made more difficult for objects that disappear completely from view. Before a hidden object can be found, the child must have a memory for the object itself, a sense of spatial locations, and a knowledge of the "nesting" properties of space (inside, underneath, on top of, etc.). This ability matures in the last three months of the first year. The search for an object that is out of sight (under a cover) is part of a special knowledge to which Piaget has given the name of "object or person permanence." In a manner analogous to the infant's discovery of the continuous existence of objects that are hidden from view is the nine-to-twelve month infant's memory of the mother as a separate person who endures and whose return after absence can be predicted.

The transition from sensory-motor activity to thinking or from the integration of practical experience into correspondingly comprehensive mental processes is the accomplishment of the first 18 to 20 months of life. By the age of two years, new mental skills emerge as the child becomes capable of "representative" thinking. He can now use symbols and signs for expression and communication. Though the first words and identified scribbles are but crude approximations compared with the stored richness of sensory-motor intelligence, they mark the beginning of a mental life going beyond action. The child is now able to transform energy and intent into ideas, dreams, and imaginative elaboration of his own constructions.

We can now trace this transition—from action to thought and from experience to knowledge—in children's discovery, understanding, and representation of the concepts of space itself. Space for the very young child consists of boundaries and limits that are known from active involvement and discovery. A child becomes familiar with space, for example, when he rides a tricycle around and around a yard, or when he runs back and forth across a room or down a passageway, or when he squeezes his body through a tunnel and emerges at the other end. Awareness of boundaries in space is here intimately connected with bodily movement and the one belongs to the other. The body in space is like a chicken in an egg, a bird in a cage, or a caterpillar on a leaf. No grid system is required for this knowledge since the space is defined by the boundaries and the surface enclosed. Within space, however, there are interfaces and juxtapositions of objects—one object beside, upon, and even inside the other, with the boundaries of the space they occupy either implicit or actual.

Spatial knowledge is reflected in the children's drawings. They will arrive at a simple conceptual schema for the things they wish to draw—trees, horses, cars, people and animals. However, depicting these objects becomes a kind of shorthand since what is represented gives overt expression to what is only a fraction of the thoughts, images, and associations invested by children in the process of representation. Conversation or stories with an understanding adult about their drawings will reveal the extent to which they are coding information and making the drawing into a kind of record of their deeper knowledge and feelings.

At the next stage, from about the ages four to seven years, the static and topological placement of objects gives way to a new awareness of movement and relative size. Children now become interested in the trajectory of movement. They indicate the projection of moving forms and can enlarge or reduce their drawings in some kind of rough scale. This is all vividly reflected in play and in their artwork. They draw or enact with dramatic gesture and movement an imitation of what they have seen—the car swerving around a bend, the bomb falling from an airplane. In sand they make waterfalls and rivers and set up to scale little towns and country scenes or battlefields in which they move all the toy people and animals around with lifelike accuracy.

Blank spaces in drawings which hitherto had not been given any function (since space was only defined in relation to the space occupied by the object) the child artist now fills with representations of movement: spirals of swirling smoke, the curved trajectory of something falling, rain descending in vertical strokes, or a series of dots to represent footprints winding along a snowy path. In this stage, children see movement as a part of the animate and inanimate world and show it in drawings quite objectively.

Is it perhaps at this stage that the child's experience of himself often becomes enmeshed in the life and movement of all that lies around? The exciting world enters his being through his sense perceptions. Conscious boundaries between self and object or person with whom there is an identification often become blurred and tenuous. Is it this that promotes the child's vivid imagination, his animistic beliefs conjured up in thought, and his sense of unity with the surroundings? Is it at this stage that a child becomes highly susceptible to the world of magic in myths and fairy tales?

This brings us to the question of how the child reaches an adequate differentiation of himself from places and people. Piaget asserts that the child's confusion (between self and other) prevents him from understanding what it is like to view the world from the viewpoint of another person or from another position in space. To understand these differing perspectives, the child must be able to distinguish right from left, up from down, and behind from in front — not as points in relation to himself, but as interrelated properties found in all orientations outside himself. This knowledge gives the child a sense of the world's three-dimensional solidity and lends *identity and permanence* to people and objects within it.

The network of relationships that can be more fully grasped is now retained in a system of thinking that is logical and objective. Piaget refers to this as the Copernican revolution in thought. The child is not now the sole center of the universe but is aware of other centers. A mental capacity emerges to bridge the space and share the thought of another in a process greatly enhanced by language (Piaget, 1948).

The play, games, drawings, and imaginative life of the child become fuller and richer. Drawings include people and animals in profile with two-dimensional limbs and features. Conservation between people or other interchanges and relationships are depicted. There are crowd scenes and street scenes in which larger, nearer figures mask the smaller figures that stand behind. The whole scene suggests a relationship between and the landscape and the relative parts of the scene are well distributed within the framework.

The Logic of Classes

Much the same story can be told developmentally in the stages by which children construct conceptual categories for the classification of objects in a group. In a well-known test of early logic (Inhelder, 1964), Piaget gives the child a number of small toys, asking him "to put together things that belong together" or "things that are alike." At an early stage, children group objects by similarities of color, form, and size equivalent to the early stage of drawing objects without relation to space. Later, children develop a notion of "belonging" heavily dependent on spatial connectedness. They will place fences, trees, animals, and houses together because they conceptualize a place like a farm or a zoo. Only from about seven years onwards do they classify objects in verbal categories, for example in classes of animal, vegetable, or mineral. The "belonging" consists of a set of characteristics that define a class of objects and distinguish that class from other classes. As in very early childhood, when the child can fit a series of boxes or eggs one within the other according to size, so now he becomes aware of the relation of "parts" to "wholes." Different degrees of inclusiveness of systems of classification become clear in the child's mind, and from about seven or eight years on, his thinking acquires a new flexibility. For example, he can now say that the fish is an animal and since there are many other kinds of animals there must be more animals in the world than fish.

Time — Order, Duration, and Speed

Closely connected with emerging *logic* and with increasing objectivity in conceptualizing *space* is the child's development of a *time* concept. This complex idea contains notions of "successive order," "duration," and "speed." Let us again indicate some of the developmental transitions in the child's thinking in this area.

The little child has difficulty with visualizing objects in space when they are moved around to new positions. In a game of hiding toys under box lids or cups, he will look in the place where the object was first hidden each time. The infant watching the mother vanish through the door will look is a puzzled way at the space beside the crib where the mother had just been standing. Does he think that she will reappear by some magic if he keeps his eyes fixed on the spot? Or is he confused about the "before" and "after" sequence of the mother's (or the hidden objects') movements?

For three-year-olds, there are similar problems. The serial *order* of three or four colored beads rolled through a tube is guessed by them to reappear in the same order that they went in. By the age of five, however, children can predict this order when the tube is tilted both forwards and backwards. If the tube is reversed (with the beads inside) through 180° back and 180° forward, the child of six or seven years can only predict the order of the beads as they come out of the tube if he is given some trials in which to correct his errors. Finally, at about seven years, the child will understand serial order and give all the right answers. He will also be able to give the right reasons (Piaget, 1969a, 1970).

If a test is given for the understanding of the related notion of *speed,* there is again confusion in preschool children. For example, a bead is rolled through each of two tunnels, one perceptably longer than the other, and made to enter and reappear at the same moment. When asked which traveled faster, the five or six-year-old will say that they went equally fast. They appear to cling to this judgment even when they can see the objects as they travel inside the tunnels. At about seven years, they no longer confuse simultaneous arrival with equally fast movement and they reason out the answer correctly. The preschool child gradually learns to take into account the relation of "duration" with "distance traveled." When he can do this at about seven or eight years, he no longer confuses "first" with "in front" or "behind" or "longer time" with traveling "farther." He can then understand the problem in a well-known test of intelligence that asks the child what he would do if on the way to school he found he was going to be late. The child of seven or eight years will be able to answer logically. He no longer "centers" on notions of distance, but he sees speed of movement as a more inclusive and simultaneous integration of the factors of time and distance.

Communication — Language, Speech, Drawing

Symbols are important for communication. *Language* includes the mental understanding of verbal symbols and syntax as well as *speech,* which is the ability to use spoken communication. Though clearly related, these aspects of human behavior are not always in a one-to-one relationship.

Though we usually conceive of language as a tool of social communication and exchange of knowledge, this is probably only its higher development. In childhood, both social and non-social aspects occur. A delicate balance also exists between the child's ability to use speech intelligibly and to relate what he thinks with what he says. It is likely that, on the one hand, logical thought shapes both language and speech, but also, on the other, that the intellect is widened by the extended world of group experience that the use of language and speech makes possible.

Looking briefly at the evolution of language through early childhood, we see that articulation begins with the first cries and vocalizations in infancy. Infants vocalize spontaneously, for example, when left alone after waking, feeling relaxed after food, or when involved in looking at their own reflection in a mirror. Then there occurs a phase of differentiation of speech sounds — phonemes begin to be shaped by imitation. A parent responds imitatively to the infant's sounds and the infant "hears" (perceives) the sound he has made and changes his own utterances to blend with what he has perceived. Single words follow, expressing an emotion, a wish, or a general observation. As these words begin to define objects or people by name, we say that the infant has the beginnings of a vocabulary. From about 14 months to the end of the second year, the construction of two- and three-word sentences begins. These sentences have a telegraphic simplicity that suits the social communication of the child of this age with his egocentric mind — "me want," "me too," etc.

Language and speech are learned by association, by imitation, and by the shaping processes of trial and error. It is probable, however, that the structural units of thought — memory images, gestures, symbolized feelings (dreams and symbolic play) and reasoning — contribute most vitally to language development. When these forms of representative thinking develop, how does a child communicate?

The child of early preschool age often speaks in monologue. His social communication is limited by the degree of his social understanding. Monologues, therefore, are explained by the "Geneva school" as another manifestation of egocentricity. Spoken language, in this phase, lacks proper syntax and the speaker may confuse the boundaries of self and other. When complex ideas evolve in his mind or when he is given directives, the child's own speech and his ability to understand others lack sophistication. He can thus use monologue to rehearse reciprocal interchanges — as in play — with himself as the referent. He can also assume that his monologue is overheard and it is, therefore, a quasi-social communication. Childlike monologues also have another quality. The child talks to himself as an older person might think verbally. Monologues are possibly, then, an initial stage towards the formation of verbal thought (Vigotsky, 1962). Studies show a decrease in this form of speech as the child reaches school age, so that monologues, like dreams, fantasy, and symbolic play, are likely to represent the imbalance of introversion characteristic of three-year-olds. At four to five years, children become more sociable and extroverted and so this imbalance is generally corrected and speech becomes more social.

What relationship has the child's drawing to language, speech, or play? *First,* it appears that speech and drawing have common elements in that both lie on a psychological continuum between expression of very personal feelings (symbolic play) and the pursuit of objectivity (imitation). *Second,* symbolic play, which uses any object to represent people or things, distorts the world at will to enhance inner feeling and fantasy. It is never the child's intention in this form of play to put objects to their proper use. They are but props with which to play out purely imaginative creations. Using line in drawing is a little different since the figurative image itself is a concrete form that modifies the intangible quality of fantasy. *Third* (related to the above), the child draws what he *knows* rather than what he actually perceives so that, as he matures, the cognitive distortions in drawings (briefly discussed in this chapter) derive more from the average child's efforts toward a balanced depiction of inner and outer reality than from purely subjective fantasy (Piaget, 1969b). This can also be said of spoken language. It seems then that child art springs from, and is a product of, the child's total inner and outer experience — as is language. It reveals levels of development in self image and in the child's mental constructs of space, time and casual relations. It also describes ongoing experiences of the outer world of home and school — the passing show captured briefly in graphic forms. *Fourth,* the not inconsiderable element of performance determines the quality of drawing and speech. Vision and manual skill or the coordination of hearing with the sensitive processes of breath, tongue, and lips enter into the child's production to influence what he *does* with his particular gift either for graphics or words.

Finally, child art and speech represent aspects of age-appropriate ego competence. An attempt at realistic drawing and adult forms of speech, though sometimes possible in gifted young children, suggests mechanical and impersonal aspects of development that are not generally characteristic of the behavior of the young child. Children draw and talk with fluid spontaneity and zest, artlessly blending fantasy and ego and feelings and perception in many different ways.

The highly individualized quality of children's art work is a reflection of a self-regulatory principle of growth. Their drawings have a unique place in their development. Like other aspects of behavior, the stage-to-stage changes in their drawings are multi-determined. Changes in content and form in their art arise out of the living processes by which children make contact with the world. They must understand what they experience and in turn allow this understanding to guide them into new discoveries and learning. The role of the parent and teacher is therefore to preserve a normal, good environment and also provide enhancing opportunities for the child's work while not directing its content or unduly influencing its form.

REFERENCES

Erickson, E.H. *Identity, Youth and Crisis*, New York: Norton, 1968.

Inhelder, B. and J. Piaget, *The Early Growth of Logic in the Child,* New York: Harper & Row, 1964.

Piaget, J. *The Child's Conception of Time* (1927). London: Routledge, Kegan Paul, 1969*a*.

Piaget, J. *The Child's Conception of Movement and Speed* (1946). London: Routledge, Kegan Paul, 1970.

Piaget, J. and B. Inhelder, *The Child's Conception of Space* (1948). New York: Norton, 1967.

Piaget, J. and B. Inhelder, *The Psychology of the Child,* (1966). New York: Basic Books, 1969*b*.

Vigotsky, L.S. *Thought and Language,* Cambridge, Mass.: The MIT Press, 1962.

Winnicott, D.W. *The Family and Individual Development.* London: Tavistock Pub., 1965.

Part Two

What Children Draw and Paint, and Why

Module One

What Do

Anything that walks, swims, or flies; lives under the ground or in the skies; can be seen, heard, felt, or smelt, may appear in children's pictures. Nothing is too large or small, too near or far, too obvious or mysterious to escape attention or demand expression.

Even when children produce nothing but scribbles and shapes, they are trying to express their observations, perceptions, feelings, and thoughts about their lives. What very young children do at this time, before they are able to make understandable forms, is usually utterly incomprehensible to adults. Their drawings and paintings are primitive and underdeveloped, but sometimes children make comments or give titles to their efforts that help adults penetrate the meaning of the mysterious markings. At other times, only prolonged study of their picture activities can provide clues to their intentions. And there is intent, even if not design, in what seems only random tracery.

When children have developed pictorial schemata — that is, shapes that have some identifying characteristics—then adults can see what the children are trying to say. The child may make a roundish contour and inside it some dots and lines. To this contour he may attach two lines downwards. For him, this signifies "person." For a student of development in child art, this initial, primitive unit of drawing has been termed a "head-man."

PEOPLE

People are the number one subject for most children's drawings. For many children, the favorite subject is themselves. Jim showed his preoccupation with himself when he pictured himself on his bicycle saying:

Children Picture?

"I am Jim—I am riding my bike, a two-wheeler—I am six years old in March—I am running a race." For almost every child, his family and his own role in the family are the most interesting subjects. Anne sketched

When Lori was three years, eight months old, she drew "Daddy" on a crumpled piece of paper. "Daddy" has no body, only legs, feet, and arms, one with a multifingered hand. His face has eyes, nostrils, and a mouth as large as the lower contour of his face. Hair is scribbled all around.

her father and mother repeatedly, but she also made drawings of "Brother and Sister," stressing this relationship without saying whether she referred to her own brother and sister.

Of the thirty children whose work appears in this book, all drew people at an early age. Ananda commented on one drawing, "I like to play with my cousins and friends." Without her remark, no one could have guessed at the figures and their activity. Maria drew people continuously but did not indicate that they belonged to her family or even were friends. Maya, four and one-half years old, made thirty drawings of people in one single day, showing in episodes all that happened when her sister Carma was born: mother, father, baby, nurses, and hospital staff.

For some children, drawing people is a consuming interest that extends into school age. Erin made people the center of her subject matter. She

When Erin was four and one-half, she drew this "Mean Old Lady" with a vertical frown, eyes set so closely together that they touch, and a crooked snarling mouth. The "lady" holds a whip in one hand, while the other huge hand threatens a dog. A boy behind her seems to cheer.

portrayed them as "characters" at an age when most children draw people all looking more or less alike, more like symbols than human beings.

For other children, people are of secondary importance. Catharine drew people as part of a larger context when they were necessary to explain an interesting activity. People may be of less interest to those children who take a special interest in animals, plants, or machines or in making fanciful pictures that reveal sensations or feelings.

For examples of children's art showing their early art with people as the main subject, view MEDIAPAK 1, frames 1-17.

ANIMALS

(A)* Some children would rather draw animals than anything else. They may draw animals and animals for months and months, even for years. Then there are children who only occasionally make drawings of animals. Some young children may portray just one animal alone, as they might draw a human portrait. Anne did this with her pet raccoon, Allan with his octopus, Kim with a dolphin, and Maria with bees.

Kim drew with feltpens groups of animals in their natural surroundings. At three years, six months, she drew "Flipper" jumping with the arching movement of dolphins.

*Boldface letters in parentheses opening a paragraph indicate the point at which to begin reading after viewing a portion of the MEDIAPAK/audiovisual program.

Young children try to make quite detailed pictures of the animal world. Sometimes these less-than-realistic shapes are self-explanatory, but at other times the meaning of the drawing and the child's feeling about this subject are difficult to understand.

It is curious how many children intensely observe bugs, bees, butterflies, or spiders, and draw them very large as though seen through a magnifying glass. Their interest and self-acquired knowledge of details lead them to draw these small creatures out of all proportion to their surroundings in nature. Catharine took a loving interest in garden "pests." Even at age nine she still made various bugs as centers of a decorative pattern.

From age three or four on, sometimes earlier, children picture birds, cats, dogs, and horses as friends and equals. Their drawings indicate a belief that animals are not much different from humans, especially themselves. They may put animals in a picture to show their own personal relationship to the animal or the animal's relationship to humans in general. Girls in particular like to draw horses because they cherish the dream of owning a horse and seem to enjoy horses more than other pets. Cheri, who stood out among young children and later among all children in her art ability, made hundreds of drawings and paintings of horses. She even was able to characterize them by breed, yet she endowed them with expression of human intelligence and humor. A rather shy and quiet child, her inner liveliness came through in her engaging animal pictures.

For examples of children's art related to animals, view MEDIAPAK 1, frames 18-31.

PLANTS

(B) Children observe plants closely and delight in them. Claude and Paul watched carefully from day to day the unfolding of plants and the insects that visted them.

Even at the early scribble stage, many children are interested in growing things, but their ways of telling about them differ. Very early they devise flower- and treelike pictures. Gradually they develop details of plant shapes and characterize tree, leaf, and blossom. Julie did not "talk" in drawings as volubly as her machine-loving brother David did, but what she told in pictures of plants makes one aware that a small child, by size alone, can get much closer to plants and observe them from nearer the ground.

At first, children show the sky-reaching height of a tree by a vertical, the tree-trunk, crossed by undifferentiated horizontals, the branches—similar perhaps to a child's feeling of his upright body with arms extended out to the sides. For Catharine, trees must have had a special personal significance. Her interest in them led her to a diversified tree vocabulary of leafy trees, candelabralike trees, slender trees, elegant trees, or compact trees.

Catharine was already a tree "specialist" at three years, five months. The top pictures here have only a sun and some blades of grass. In the middle at left, a tree trunk is crossed by horizontal branches hung with apples. At the right is a new kind of tree with an umbrella of dots for leaves and a sun overhead. In the bottom row at left, the familiar scene has a sunlit field, but at the right there is a Man.

To young children, plants seem alive not only in the adult sense of needing nourishment and making growth but animated by thoughts and feelings. In many a child's drawing, a tree or flower is humanized, shown with a face, presented as a guardian of birds, insects, mammals, even as a protector and friend of the child himself.

For examples of children's art related to plants, view MEDIAPAK 1, frames 32-40.

MACHINES

(C) Some young children prefer to draw machines and other man-made objects. Their pictures of trucks, trains, boats, rockets, airplanes, or helicopters may emerge simultaneously with their man-drawings, but sometimes come earlier. For these children, machinery has a great impact on their imagination; machines are not adjuncts to man, but man is a mere adjunct to his machines. Their drawings show a machine-oriented and machine-directed world. They may identify with the machine, enter into its spirit. We often see a child at play with a toy airplane, imitating the flight of a real plane, moving his arms, making its noise, trying to reproduce all his own sense perceptions of flying planes. David and

When David was four, he drew pictures about his family's move west. This picture, called "Ouch," is a moving train-car piled high with luggage, each piece with a smiling face. He also drew the highways on both sides, one above, the other below the train, despite the flat terrain.

Benjamin, each in a different manner, were such machine-oriented picture specialists. While David's extraordinary interest in machines of all kinds confined itself to this subject as long as he made pictures, that is until age seven, Benjamin, from three and one-half years on, gradually enlarged his interest to living things, although technical aspects continued to play a large role.

Among the very young, the technical aspects of the present world hold great fascination, but their pictures show clearly that the interpretation of one child may be quite different from that of another.

For examples from a specific case of machines drawn by one child, view MEDIAPAK 1, frames 41-51.

SENSES AND FEELINGS

(D) Human sensory experiences are of many kinds and often mixed. A train can be seen, heard, and even smelt. In fact, its passage can produce a "wind" as it displaces the air. The very young child can discriminate between what he sees, hears, smells, or touches and he often tries to express such experiences visually. For him, they are intertwined, but one may have a stronger impact than another.

He uses lines, shapes, and colors to communicate not only what is visible to him, including action and continuity of movement, but other sensory experiences, even abstract concepts and emotions. The great diversity of his experiences in the outer world becomes part of his inner world.

Children frequently use color to express sensations, especially "color happy" young ones like Maya, Lori, or Rochelle. Almost all children show in their pictures a large sun, sometimes more than one in the same picture, even a sun inside the house, to indicate they are having a nice,

Lori lives in California. To her friend Laura and other children there, rain is a great event. In this tiny pen and ink drawing, she pictures, at four years, nine months, the pleasures of "Laura and Me in the Rain."

happy day. For every child in a region of cloudless skies during many months of the year, rain, clouds, even fog are great events. Many children, like Lori or Maria, celebrated in their drawings their delight in rain, in rainbows, and in walking in the rain.

While making pictures, young children often express their feelings by saying, "I love you, Mommy" or "To Daddy, love" or their good wishes on occasions like birthdays or St. Valentine's day. In a way, this is a burst of affection that children may be embarrassed to utter in directly spoken words. When they are able to write, they may add a dedication. They may show affection by drawing flowers with smiling faces and make a present of such a picture to one they love; they may make a picture of this kind like a joke, as Benjamin did with a train put together with hearts. A child also extends expressions of devotion and brotherhood to animals and plants. Paul drew an apple-shaped house for a worm. Houses for animals only or for flowers occur also. Most adults find these fantasies puzzling and regard them as evidence of immaturity, as "childish."

RELIGIOUS FEELINGS

Some very young children express strong religious feelings in their pictures. Maya fondly portrayed her church many times. Claude, in a remarkable way, let animals display his religious feelings. Erin made many pictures showing her warm association with the church.

For examples of children's art showing sensory experiences and feelings, view MEDIAPAK 1, 52-64.

FANTASY AND IMAGINATION

(E) It is astonishing to find out from their pictures how differently very young children view the same outside world and transform it to suit their fantasies. Some children clearly show the actual appearance of the things they have observed. Others transform the real world into highly individual fantasies. The inner world of their imagination does not reflect objectively the appearance of things as the adult sees them. According to the range of their picture "vocabulary" and their ability to present an organized scene, the children frequently picture a strange and rich world of emotions, projected feelings, and imagined happenings. There is no question about the existence of the world of fantasy they create in pictures. What is in question is the readiness of adults to accept these communications and their willingness to try to understand what the child is saying.

Allan's imaginary world is filled with monsters, ghosts, and haunted houses, weird "Frankenstein" creatures, fearful scenery, and a strange

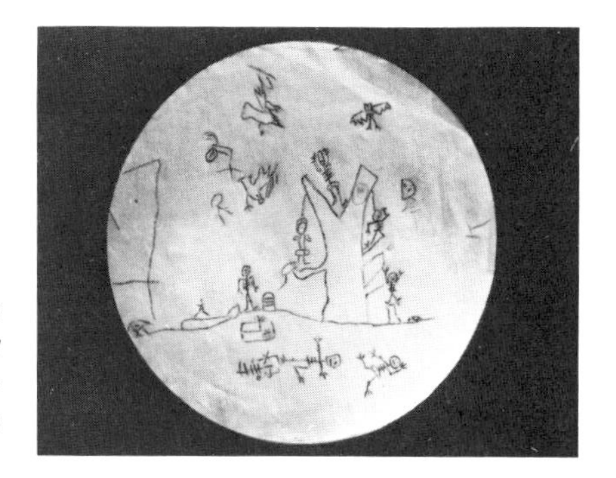

In six-year-old Allan's "Ghosts and Skeletons around Dead-Tree," the tree stands on a wavy groundline. From its stubby branches hang skeletons and the ghostly dead. At left is a cliff. In the air, bats and vultures circle and dive.

underground world. Anne's wide-ranging imagination influenced her many picture stories from the time she was three and one-half years old. When she learned how to write, she composed her own stories and illustrated them. She also made drawings for many fairy tales and myths. In quite a different way, Kate's imagination transformed everyday surroundings into a beautiful dream world that she put into pictures. Maria used her imagination in humorous "take-offs" on humans and their activities and in animal pictures in which she endowed her creations with human thoughts and emotions. Like many children, she could "tell all" in pictures.

For examples of children's art showing fantasy and imagination, view MEDIAPAK 1, frames 65-77.

(F) What very young children draw, and why they do it, is obscure to many adults. When children develop schemata with some identifying characteristics, then adult understanding begins. The great miracle of this expression-in-pictures is that the child helps his own development. By putting down his observations of the world around him, of himself and his relationships to others, he gains insight, clarifies his own problems, and develops an ability to solve them. Consistent with childhood and with his growth, he gives visible form to many aspects of his life. Indeed, the most direct and intense expressions are those of the very young—unspoiled, unabashed, uncompromising, they can be a revelation.

Very young children are still as one with living nature and the objects around them. They look upon their families and the entire world of animals, plants, and objects with the eyes and minds of friendly, unprejudiced, imaginative explorers.

Module Two

What is the Art

The term "art" usually denotes an extraordinary ability of forceful and unique expression for experiences of the mind and heart. It implies a high level of complex, creative, mature achievement. It refers particularly to the visual arts, but is also used to describe an exceptional level of creativity or performance in music, drama, dance, and other human endeavors. The term "artist" connotes an ability of expression different from and greater than the expressive abilities of most people. Child art, on the other hand, is applied to whatever children produce in a visual presentation, with means and materials similar to those of adult artists, regardless of whether or not the results transcend children's average performance. Child art is usually merely a record of self-expression of experience, and lacks the qualities properly associated with the term art. Therefore, the terms "child art" or "children's art" are misnomers. It is well to keep in mind that the use of the term "art" for child art is a loosely applied term, all embracing, not defined in regard to quality.

Children have many ways of expressing thoughts, feelings, observations, and judgments by means other than words (for example, play activities—the repetition of sounds and motor activities). All of these are not described indiscriminately as art, nor is their speech, unless it is of greater sensitivity and in a form more meaningful than expected on a standard child level.

The brush strokes and splotches of very young children, like the paintings of Joanna, have been hailed by adults as abstract art, as part of the variations of expressionist art of the last fifty or sixty years. When child art is viewed as belonging to the particular abstract style of this adult art, it is often given an adult interpretation, as can easily happen to Catharine's extraordinary paint-scribbles. This is unfortunate.

in Children's Art?

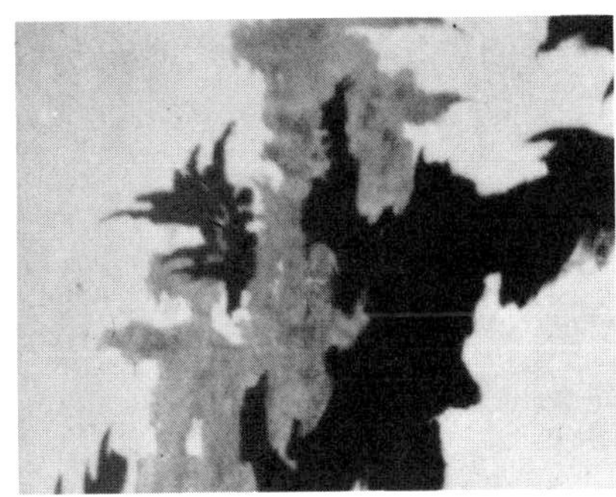

At age three, Joanna painted (at left) separate areas of deep blue and bright red on a blue ground, with a touch of green. These separate areas have decorative and compositional design and color qualities that are well-defined. Now compare Joanna's abstract with the abstract (detail at right) by adult artist Clyfford Still. The colors are different, but the compositional concept, grouping, and irregular edges of each color part are somewhat similar.

A young child does not see or interpret abstract art as related to his own productions. This was illustrated by two and one-half-year-old Becky, quite advanced and prolific in her own picturing of figures and objects but also doing "abstracts" in ordered brush strokes and startling colors. At an exhibit of abstracts, her mother told her that these were "just as nice as pictures of *things.*" The child rejected what she saw as meaningless. Her own paintings, like one she called "Stars," picture a definite content though the effect is that of an abstract.

The adult who creates abstractions arrives at them in a disciplined manner. Realism of objective and symbolic expressionism seems unsuited for (his own) creative expression of the essence of his own experience. His presentation is a purposeful reduction to stringent and distilled shapes with no apparent resemblance to natural forms. He has carried these into abstraction of color and line. However, when one sees the sketches in the series from which an end product is evolved, the origin of the subject becomes clear. The adult abstract creation is quite beyond mere communication or expression. It is the result of conscious exploration that transcends the need for any message for the viewer.

The child's way is just the opposite of this procedure. From seemingly abstract form, he strives toward realism, limited by the level of picturing ability he has reached. Catharine, only three and one-half years old, was not able to paint realistically, but some of her achievement has artistic merit. A child can be considered truly an artist when he has achieved discipline of line, color, arrangement, when his art reflects a controlled emotional content, when his message has a visual form that exercises an impact. Only then is a child's pictorial effort an expression with its own artistic values. At this point it is truly the *art* of the child. Claude used simple means, but had astonishing control of these means.

A child's art must not be confused with adult art or compared with it. It must not be compared with tribal art that is evolved from a long and meaningful tradition. The child's art must not be related to an adult art that is entirely devoid of any allusion to living or man-made shapes. The child's art is differently inspired. A realistic meaning underlies the child's abstract-looking productions. Though they may seem shapeless, they represent his efforts to express the world. His struggle for shapes is related to the reality outside and within himself. What may seem formless to an adult is the child's attempt to picture people, animals, plants, objects, and the meaning these have for him. He is also expressing emotions and feelings related to his world that are strange and difficult for others to comprehend. His emotional and experiential ties with the living and with "things" are at the bottom of the urge to give them expression and shape.

Consequently, the term *art,* applied indiscriminately to children's pictorial manifestations, is confusing and questionable. But, introduction of a new terminology may also be confusing. *For this reason, and ONLY for this reason, the term child ART is retained in this program.*

Child art has a style of its own that sets it apart from any other art. All children express themselves through that style. Therefore, *its style IS childhood,* something separate from anything adult. This fact was observed and stated by Cizek, the great art educator, as early as 1912, and later in a general sense by Piaget who said, "The intellectual and moral structures of the child are not the same as ours. . . ." Furthermore, also recognized by Cizek at the turn of the century, is the fact that child art is not a preliminary stage leading to adult art. Some of Anne's pictures show the different kind of style which is characteristic of her work and that of other children, a child's ingenious approach to rendering what he experiences.

The few adult artists of whose great ability in childhood we know actually reached adulthood in their art during childhood. As an example, consider Giovanni di Paolo, the remarkable painter who, while still a young child, produced art of adult quality in the days of the early Renaissance. He was like Mozart, that incredibly precocious child-musician of a later century, an adult in music while still a child in years. In their art they ceased to be children.

Unfortunately, most children whose art is considered remarkable do not carry on their extraordinary ability. They may stop doing art entirely and turn their main life interests to other pursuits. In some cases, they salvage their childhood ability in the form of crafts or art interests or perhaps a greater understanding and judgment in matters of taste and art.

The style of child art may remind us of certain kinds of adult art in other parts of the world or in other times, but there is no doubt that it is distinguished from all adult art by specific characteristics. It is candid in the sense of being frank, simple, untaught, showing experiences as seen through the child's eyes. Child art may seem naive, yet the child shows his knowledge about his world. Jennifer's drawings show an appraising and "knowing" interpretation of people and situations. A child may seem to lack sophistication yet, on the nonadult level, he quite often has sophistication. Again, what is essential to him does not always coincide with the adult's concept of essentials. Representation of essentials goes hand in hand with simplification, another characteristic of the style of child art. Furthermore, it defines itself by the distinct, though unconscious freedom from adult traditions.

When Maya Pines says in an article quoting Professor White that "one-year-olds spend more than one-fifth of their waking hours 'gaining information by looking', that is, staring at various things intently as if to memorize their features," we should add that this immobility, like a frozen attention, also must include information by listening. During this and the second year, while crawling on all fours, the small child gains information from touching, smelling, and tasting things.

When a child selects his subjects for picture making, he may not be too influenced by purely visual aspects of his subjects. He creates a "reification" (to use an apt term of Herbert Read) of his observations and sensations which may not be comprehensible to the adult. The child finds ways to translate such intangibles as things heard, touched, smelled, or in motion into visual language. One can observe this early in Becky's pictures.

Speculative as it may sound, there also is no doubt that early child art is an emotional projection. The intensity of this projection may vary considerably. Yet, love and fear, admiration, wonder, amazement, and any number of other experiences of this nature are "discussed" or recorded by children in their pictures. Adult artists also express emotions, even in apparently purely descriptive pictures, either directly or by way of circumscription. But the differences and limitations of the adult's and the child's world condition the profound "otherness" of both. *Child art is not a junior adult art.*

A number of characteristics cause one to associate children's pictures with those of adults in an effort to understand them. Resemblances that are striking exist only in part. For example, in the early or archaic periods of Western or Oriental "fine arts," in the pre-Renaissance or early classical periods, there appear details that have their startling rebirth in child art far away in time and place. There are more direct similarities to folk art. A catalogue to a Swiss Folk Art Exhibit states: " . . . *folk* art has nothing to do with *'art'* in the accepted sense of the word . . . does not have to meet aesthetic standards; being a part of *folklore* it has to be judged by criteria that pertain to this *branch of knowledge.*"* This statement lends itself remarkably well to child art when paraphrased: "*child* art has nothing to do with *adult* art . . . being a part of *childhood* it has to be judged by criteria that pertain to this *branch of knowledge—childhood.*"

Children often represent certain plants, animals, and objects very much as they appear in adult folk art when these parts are isolated from the rest of the total picture. The child's schema and some forms of folk art

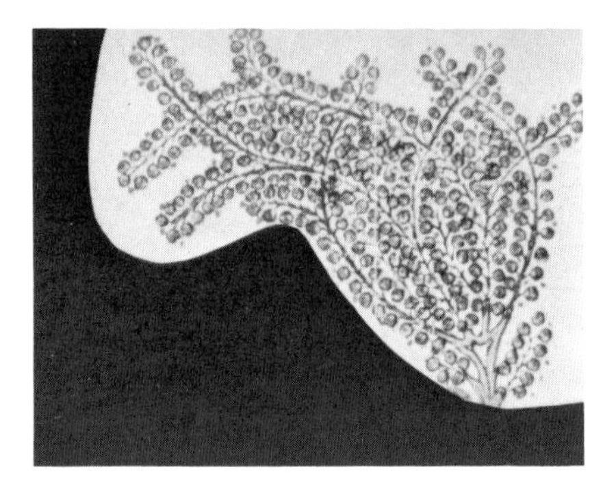

Five-year-old-Claude (at left) used a single leaf form and repeated it exactly for all the leaves of his tree. He employed unrealistic colors and the same contoured shape for all. In the page (at right) from a 13th century manuscript of Islamic art are leaves and branches of the tree, endless repetitions of one simplified leaf shape. This pictorial concept is very similar to that used by Claude and many other children who seem to represent many plants, animals, or objects as they are depicted in folk art. In the context of their entire compositions, however, similarities of style are found only in some details and in the "naive" approach.

*Italics by author.

have the same simplified shapes. Claude, Paul and other children in this study show it in their drawings and paintings, perhaps particularly in the representation of leaves of trees. During some very sophisticated periods of oriental art, the mantle of tree leaves or needles, brush drawn, and the branch structure that shows between, have such similarities. Childlike types of trees appear in Swedish and Swiss folk art, in Islamic paintings, or in modern work. To represent a group of trees or a small woods, children and sometimes adults render the same type of tree, repeated over and over, their group arrangements remarkably alike.

In the case of animals, the details of feathers or of fish scales or the curly wool of a sheep's fleece seem to repeat what either folk art or tribal art or Western art of the twelfth and thirteenth centuries carefully and lovingly executed in their textural patterns. This applies equally to the representation of human hair, taken by itself apart from the face it frames. Both child and adult artist make the same single hair or curl in endless repetitions with the difference that the child does not achieve the calculated, cumulative effect of the adult. On the surface, details may seem quite similar, yet when inspected closely, differences clearly appear.

There are also certain resemblances in the manner of grouping. Children, especially in early drawings, align figures and objects in a manner quite like pictographs. However, the single figures in adult pictographs are not executed in a child's manner. Images of people in such adult, folk, or tribal art differ perceptibly from the child's human schema. Children's maplike space arrangements that favor complete or partial bird's-eye views

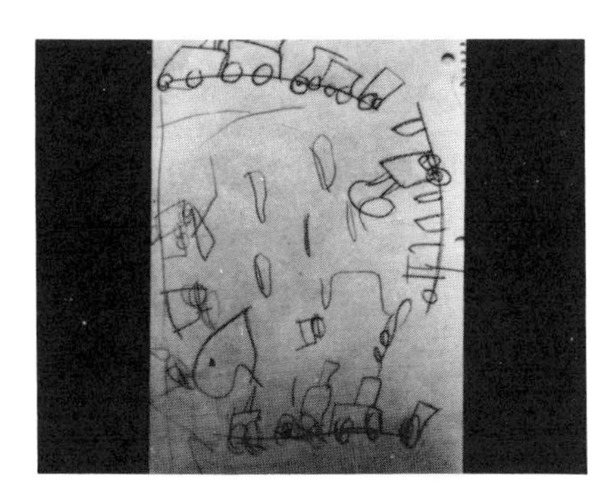

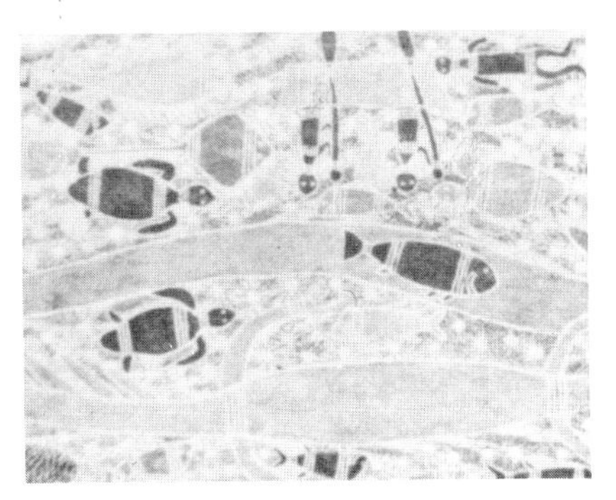

Benjamin, aged twenty-eight months, made a maplike layout of tracks surrounding a body of water and trains stand on the tracks in side-views. The boats are indicated by mere shapes. At left, a huge fish head profile appears. The spatial representation of the "Fish-Hunt" (detail at right.) by Australian aborigines is based on the same concept as that used by Benjamin and other young children. There is no single point of vantage. The maplike layout shows bodies of water and star-shaped symbols for vegetation. Boats and occupants are in front-view, paddles are vertical, fish are in profile, and turtles and crocodiles are seen from above. The difference between child and tribal artist is in the maturity and artistic capability of the latter.

come close to some aboriginal tribal or folk art, as one can see in certain pictures of the research collection on which this program is based.

In provincial and amateur art, there are also elements to which child art is linked by a strong resemblance. However, the separateness of the nature of the two kinds of art remains unmistakable. Within adult art, there are wide stylistic differences in art periods and many individual differences within periods. This is also true of children's art. At a very early age, individual differences begin to appear, each child developing his individual "style" within a style that must be termed *child art*.

For examples and discussion of child art as "art," view MEDIAPAK 2, frames 1-22.

Module Three

Young Children's

Individuality in child art does not appear suddenly, though it may become suddenly apparent to an outsider. Each child has his own characteristics, just as he has his own personality, manifested from the first day after birth in differences of response and behavior: he may be quiet or noisy, thoughtful or active, quick or slow, sociable or withdrawn. More important than these obvious signs are the intangibles, difficult to communicate at all because they belong to the child's private inner world, the center of his further growth. Art activity is one of the important ways to give expression to this inner world of childhood.

Added to the need for expression is the child's great joy in just "doing," his pleasure in the process itself as well as in what he accomplishes. Words, play, and other means do not fully express the complex feelings, the moving forces that demand some kind of outward form. Though limited by their level of development and their differences in skills in the use of materials, children are able to express amazing variety in their interpretations of similar subject matter, whether people or animals, sensations, feelings, or emotions. Their beginning art efforts and comments upon them often give valuable clues to what they cannot express in other ways. Later, they may become more inventive and expressive as they develop in representational skills. However, the results of their efforts are usually *more creative than artistic.*

Children's drawings and paintings reveal their distinctly different personalities in several ways:

1. Choice of subject and degree of emphasis on particular preferences.
2. Understanding and interpreting their own relations to humans, to other living things, and to objects; also, relations between people and between people and animals.

Individualism in Art

Each child is unique. In drawings and paintings that express children's interests and attitudes, their choices of subject reveal differences. At four years, three months, Maya drew hospital scenes like this children's ward with patients in double beds, the head nurse, and a small child.

3. Humanization of animals, plants, and even objects. Most children go through this phase but express humanization at different times and for different lengths of time.
4. Representation of various sensory perceptions and sensations.
5. Expression of emotions like love, fear, or even hate. They frequently relate them to and sometimes fixate them on a particular person, animal, or object.
6. Presentation of intangibles such as enjoyment, happiness, and spiritual needs. They often try to give a concrete form to concepts and abstract ideas.
7. Re-creation of play. Through their pictures, they relive vicariously their own play or that of other children.
8. Communication of their constant need for security, both physical and emotional. They fantasize their fears and the protection they expect from home and parents or imaginary protectors.
9. Repetition of particular picture subjects. In their individual styles, they repeat their favorite subject and techniques in long series. In these repetitions, they develop their subject until they have

Trenton made a series of "The Dragon," with the same scene in every drawing. The Dragon is always green. It rises from blue water and tries to get into the house. Like his "giant" in a drawing done earlier, the dragon is a menace, but Trenton is now seven months older and has found a way to combat the dragon.

achieved a satisfying result or exhausted its interest. They may keep going until they have mastered their subject and repetition becomes a comfortable, enjoyable game.

The combination of a variety of these characteristics leads to a recognizable style of picturing that belongs to only this one child. With enough material for observation, adults can single out the work of a particular child by his "art."

It is important to let differences happen without interference, to let them take their course. To preserve one's individuality requires self-confidence and real strength of one's inner convictions. The truth is that the child's world is not the adult's world; adults are strangers in it. You can see why this is so. Even if an adult can recall strange images or incidents that he experienced in childhood and what he thought about them, he seldom remembers the earliest, most important ones. Furthermore, even those occasional flashes of adult insight into the young child's world remain on a level of non-identification. The experience might be compared with that of a stranger in a distant tribal community; he may be an observer, even a participant, but not an initiate in sacred ceremonies. He may be knowledgeable and empathic, but he cannot fully understand the ceremonies because he is unable to identify with the experiences and outlook of the tribe. Adult deductions and explanations, even when based on repeated observations, may be erroneous because they are made from a *non-child perspective.*

Although adults cannot really enter into the child's inner world, they are in control of his outer world. It is important to watch, to listen, to try to learn from the child's efforts at expressing himself. It is equally important to encourage the child, to provide opportunity, and allow time for him to find his own way. When the child does find a way of expression that satisfies him, he will need time and freedom to enjoy it. Before language can serve as a bridge between child and adult, art activities provide an avenue of communication.

A child's drawings may seem mysterious, but sometimes the immediate situation or event may supply a clue. The child's comments may help.

Sometimes, when questioned, he will readily explain what he has said in his drawing. At other times he may have started out without any idea, or an idea he did not carry through. The very act of drawing may itself pro-

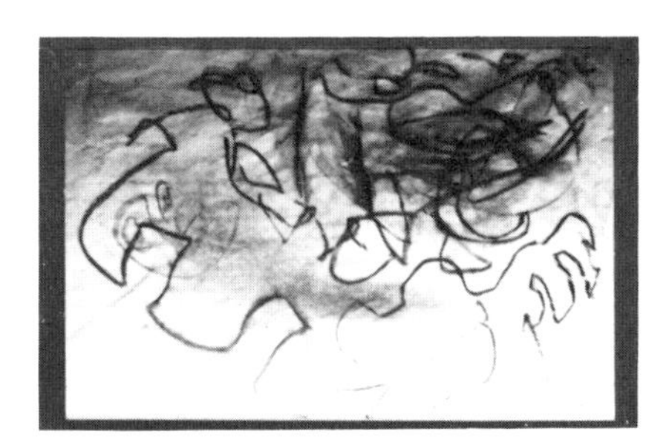

At four, Rochelle announced that she was going to make a "horse." Its profile faces left. Look for the ears on top, a very indistinct eye, a big nose, a large, square, open mouth and a square chin. Just below the chin, she drew a stubby short leg. Then (at right) Rochelle turned her paper bottom to top. Seen this way it now must have looked to Rochelle like stairs, because she added some steps at the left and called her picture "Crooked Stairs."

duce a change; what appears on the page may cause him to change his mind, or he may forget what he planned. Sometimes he simply may not want to open the door to his inner world and may substitute an explanation which is not the real one.

For examples of individualism in child art, view MEDIAPAK 2, frames 23-47.

(A) In spite of these almost unsurmountable obstacles toward understanding a child's early art efforts, a constant awareness will be rewarded by growing appreciation of what this activity means to the child.

Children need to be entirely secure within the direction given by their own natures. Attention, encouragement, perhaps praise, quite often the spontaneous delight of parents with their child's achievements, represent the unchanging love and security of home.

Children may be more limited at home in materials to work with, but they can experiment, repeat, and explore their interests to their own satisfaction. Similar to the adult who sometimes needs quiet and seclusion for reflection, so the very young child also requires quiet and privacy to discover and develop his own individual way of "seeing" himself.

Self-portraits offer amazing manifestations of children's exploration of the self at very young ages. They are, of course, a self-affirmation, a way of showing self-esteem, but also of questioning who or what they are. A child's portraiture is severely limited by his ability to reflect an interpretation of his own person. He certainly gives thought to his own image, what he thinks of himself,or what he hopes to look like. His investigation is related to his development and his opinion of himself. The adult artist is affected

Jill portrayed herself at three years, ten months with a large mouth and her hair carefully styled.

by similar factors. Most of the children represented in this program did self-portraits. Only a few, like David or Maria, were *not* interested in portraying themselves. Some, like Norena, had not yet developed past the stage of mere shapes.

For examples of children's self-portraits, view MEDIAPAK 2, frames 48-65.

(B) Case by case, each very young child shows he is a unique being in the differences of his picturing from that of others. The "average" child and his art is a fiction of statistical invention. He does not exist in reality. However, despite individual differences, each child shares the stages of his development with all other children in the world. Knowledge of this amazing universality is an excellent basis for observing the individual child's growth. As each child develops, he has his own special way of moving through these universal stages. No matter how carefully made, statistical cross-sectional studies of children's picturing according to age levels or by the timing of their developmental phases take insufficient notice of each child's separateness. These differences are so much part of his individuality that he maintains them almost like physical characteristics. To better understand the significance of such differences and to give all children encouragement and more time for undisturbed early art expression should be definite goals of child study.

Similarities in children's art have been the basis of comparative measurements and evaluations of children's intelligence, maturation, and normalcy. The results have stressed likenesses within a given developmental stage. Noticeable deviations from established norms tend to be interpreted as indicators of brightness or retardation, of problems or degrees of mental disturbances, etc. Parents interested in their own children's development, their learning habits, and manner of expression and behavior sometimes consult these published investigations. They may find reassurance when some phenomenon that intrigues or worries them is reported as a normal, though transitional, part of behavior. Normalcy is sometimes confused with "average" or conformity within a group. However, there is adequate range within "normalcy" for the healthy differences between individuals.

Individuality, in its growth and development, is an affirmation of identity in a person. Through all changes, it confirms essentially his own uniqueness. A child's individuality will be visible in his physique, his behavior, and his expression of feelings. The art of the very young may show some aspects of his personality that other activities may not reveal.

Part Three

How Do Young Children Draw and Paint?

Module Four

General Course of

Ever since art historian Corrado Ricci "discovered" children's art and wrote about it in the 1880s, the subject has been investigated the world over. The main body of most studies endeavors to explain how children represent the tangible world in their drawings and paintings. There is no doubt about the importance of this aspect of child art since the course of its development appears to be the same for all children everywhere.

Ninety years of inquiries have shown that children's art development proceeds in successive stages. Although related to chronological age, it is not narrowly dependent on it, and although related to mental age, this relation appears to be significant in only a limited number of aspects.

We can roughly identify three main stages of development: SCRIBBLE, SCHEMA, and TRUE-TO-APPEARANCE.

The first of these, the *scribble stage,* is distinguished by an assembly of lines, several or many, short or long, traced in all kinds of ways and directions: straight, curved, zig-zagging, circular, angular, hooked, or scalloped.

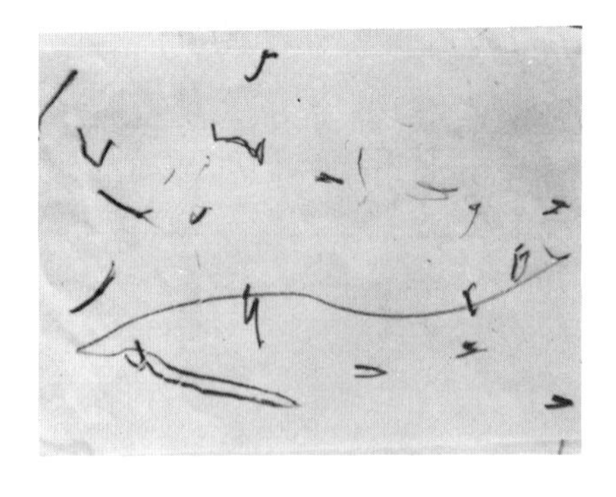

Valerie, at twenty-five months, made these short lines and dots. At the bottom, a long line leads to a closed shape which she called a "Boat."

Children's Art Development

These scribbles are the product of physical activity that the child enjoys and probably needs. They are evidence of the child's curiosity and his exploring mind. Scribbles develop into *shapes* that cannot be identified

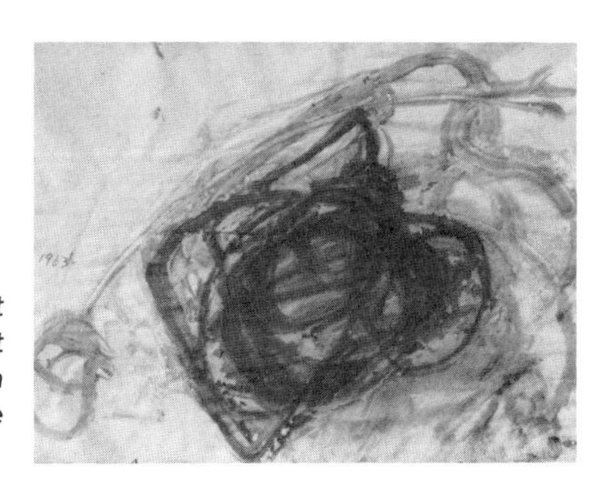

Two years old, John first painted scribbles that led to a roundish shape that he filled with paint of the same color, creating a shaded patch with ragged contours. To it, he added a miniature shape, as if held by string to the larger shape.

with known objects. Gradually, some shapes become partly, then increasingly identifiable.

For examples of scribbles and shapes, view MEDIAPAK 3, frames 1-10.

(A) In the *preschematic phase* that follows scribbles and shapes, part of the object is recognizable and serves as a *primitive schema.* The lumpish shape of a head by itself with dots for eyes and a line for the mouth means "man." When provided with legs, it becomes a "head-man." A vertical line intersected by horizontals means "tree." A box-like enclosure with odd rounds and squares set inside at irregular intervals may mean "house."

Ananda, at four, made primitive figures. Here she says, "I Like to Go to the Store with My Two Pennies." Her enormous left hand has many fingers and two round pennies on its palm.

The *schema* is characterized by definite outlines of parts of figures or objects that are assembled in a manner sufficiently real to suggest what it is meant to represent. Some parts or details by themselves may not be identifiable, while others have qualities that facilitate identification. With a single characteristic that distinguishes it from just any "bird," like the beak of a duck, the child makes his schema more specific. Gradually, he increases the number of schemata and develops each to show its identity among other schemata of the same kind. The young child may select for each member of the family an attribute for this person alone, size, hair style, or favorite garment. The schematically drawn person or object may be by itself or placed among shapes as yet unrecognizable.

Finally, the young child has developed a schematic vocabulary. He may reach a point when he can represent almost anything he wishes in schematic forms recognizable to the viewer. Of the thirty children studied in this program, Maria and Anne developed a great variety of schemata ready to serve their needs. The child's astuteness in choosing *pictorially intelligible* characteristics makes his schematic representation easy for communicating what he wishes to say. With his assessment of the essence of

A well-developed schema may differ from a less developed one by the number of details, clarity of arrangement, decor, or other qualities. Maria, at six and one-half, made these completely worked-out schemata of "Mother, Child, and Dog." They are entirely recognizable and clear.

the subject, he seems to stabilize his knowledge of his environment and satisfy himself in his relation to it. This ability also enables a child to transcend picture communication of the concrete world and express his sensations, emotions, humor, even his judgments. A few children are able to give their pictures aesthetic qualities of arrangement, simplification, decoration, or color.

For examples of primitive schemata and schematic pictures, view MEDIAPAK 3, frames 11-24.

(B) All schemata have some observable single characteristics peculiar to the nature of schematic representation. One of them is *lack of proportion.* The head of a figure is usually too large in proportion to the rest of the figure, often unusually so, even as large as the remaining figure. Legs may be as short as stumps (head-man) or as long as stilts (leg-man). Small parts like fingers may be exaggerated, made disproportionately large or small. Entire limbs may be omitted, as in a one-armed figure.

Another phenomenon used by many young children is *transparency.* The child reveals something he knows to exist but that is invisible at the time or in the view he is drawing. He may draw a person's body seen through his clothes, the rooms and furniture of a house seen through the walls, or the baby inside his mother.

For examples of lack of proportion, transparency, and pregnancy, view MEDIAPAK 3, frames 25-38.

(C) Still another characteristic is the child's representation of *three-dimensional space,* of bodiness. He puts on the top of his drawing page a house that is in the distance and places at the bottom persons that are near. House and people are one above the other and all of the same size.

Naomi, at four years, ten months, titled this picture "Story." A man with a dog is shown in front-view at the top of the picture. They are behind the house and trees which are shown in the mid-section. A walk, shown in bird's-eye view and looking like a ladder, leads down to the house and tree, which are shown in elevation on a groundline. In front of the house is a fenced-in garden space with a man lying on the grass. Though shown horizontally, the man is drawn as if seen from above. This scene represents the distance between the near foreground of the fence to well behind the house.

He may try to clarify a situation by a maplike positioning of various people and objects. In developing the schema, he may draw the schematic rider above the horse and entirely separate from it. People who hold hands may barely touch each other or the hands may be separate though close.

In the primitive schematic picture, some children put several things on the same page, as Becky did at twenty-nine months. They may scatter their single objects all over the page, each seen from a different direction. Benjamin did this. As the child's representation develops, he makes a groundline or earthline on which everything stands, thus gathering them together in one direction as if viewed in a lineup.

The use of color is also developmental. Within the schematic stage, color choices at first indicate no relation to the object. The child seems to experiment arbitrarily or favors certain colors for almost everything. Eyes may be red, ears brown, hair green, the mouth blue. The young child may use colors to indicate something "new" he found out or something that he finds remarkable or simply to distinguish one person or object from another. Even in his later, fully-developed schema, he may select a color to express sensory or emotional experiences. He may explain why he used purple color for the frosting of a cake that has white icing by saying, "it tastes purple!" This is similar to another child's explanation of his picture with the sun inside a room, "It is a beautiful day." A child may use fantastic colors that make a situation so unreal that adults can only guess at the meaning. However, the schema usually is presented in "true" colors: grass is green, apples are red, water is blue. Some children, as they continue in the development of their schemata, vary these true colors: they use more than one green, red, or blue.

For examples of other schematic characteristics, view MEDIAPAK 3, frames 39-47.

(D) As they grow older, most children become aware of a disparity between their schemata and the true appearance of things. They try to create the general impression that a person or object makes on them. In drawing a tree, they try to show the whole mantle of the foliage instead

Cheri's horses and colts appear in realistic proportion, with natural movements and horse characteristics. Seven years old, she made the horse in the foreground much larger, those in the pasture small. However, tree, flowers, and sun have remained schematic.

of making innumerable single separate leaves, all alike. The conflict between their pictographic vocabulary and the appearance they wish to represent leads children into a transitional stage of picture making, a mixture between the new representation to which they aspire and their well-known former schemata.

Eventually, a *true-to-appearance* stage of representation may be reached. Proportions are drawn correctly, colors are represented truly and, frequently, in a variety of shadings. Objects hidden from a given vantage point are not shown. Space and depth are indicated as they appear from the place where the viewer stands. Objects in the foreground are drawn proportionally larger than those in the background; parallel lines, like the sides of a street, converge toward the horizon. Foreshortening, the lighted

The mastery of ***perspective*** *in drawing is characteristic of adult facility and is entirely different from the schematic space representation of a child. At age eleven, when most children still draw in schemata or strive toward adult realism, Cheri's ability had reached the level of a gifted adult. In clear perspective, she shows the interior of a stable with the horses in their stalls and a glimpse through the door.*

and shaded sides of an object, perhaps even its cast shadow are represented. The result is that one or many objects are drawn "as they appear true to life," in correct spatial positions relative to one another. The illusion of depth is created similar to a photographic picture, regardless of artistic merits.

For examples of transition to and true-to-appearance representation, view MEDIAPAK 3, frames 48-58.

(E) Few children reach the true-to-appearance stage. Indeed, nearly half of all adults never reach it and, when forced to draw, do so in a schematic or diagrammatic manner. For many children at age levels when this developmental advance would occur, verbal expression has already replaced pictorial communication. Frequently, the child ceases to make pictures. He takes up other activites in which he feels he is more successful, that are more rewarding, and perhaps more in line with the interests of his peers. Persistent as is the direction of all children's progression through the universal stages of picture development, the level they reach and the age when they reach it vary greatly. Children with strong self-criticism of their own art work often abandon spontaneous picture making during their earliest school years. Others do so in early adolescence. At this point, the frustration of not reaching the level of achievement they would like is usually the cause of their disenchantment with drawing.

No matter what and how they draw and paint, most young children seem to have an irresistible urge for pictorial communication, especially strong in the *very* young who draw on walls and furniture and disregard admonition and punishment for doing it. Why does this great drive to draw, draw, and draw disappear? And why, even when artistic ability and quality are extraordinarily high — and encouraged — does it vanish at the beginning of adolescence or even earlier, at ages seven and eight, as observed in some children in the longitudinal research presented in this program.

Module Five

The Young Child's Beginnings:

Trenton made his earliest scribbles on the furniture and on the floor. Needless to say, his mother did not keep them. From the age of fourteen months and during the first months of his scribble activity on paper, he did not produce large numbers of pictures. He distributed his scribbles sparsely on his drawing page and appeared to set them down with de-

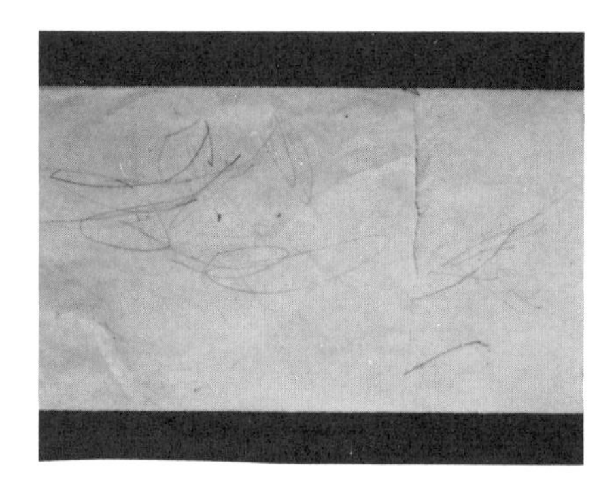

Trenton's early scribblings were often sparsely distributed, using angular lines like these, made with deliberation, at sixteen months.

liberation. He also made paint scribbles. His sister, Lori, then three and one-half years old, made paint shapes in strong colors, especially reds. Trenton worked sometimes at the same table and must have used her colors, diluting them to the more delicate pastel shades that he favored.

In general, the very young child starts with scribbled lines or brush scribbles as early as two, and "communicates" on walls, pavement, paper, any material on which he can leave a visible mark. On paper, pictures are most easily preserved and most often available for study.

To the adult, the *scribble stage* appears to be a meaningless jumble of lines, whether made by pencil, pen, color feltpens, crayons, chalk, paints,

From Scribble to Shape

Lori's "Lion" is the most fascinating of her many scribble paintings. The head (enclosed in a curly scribble for the mane) is at the right, with two close-set eyes and a triangle of nose and mouth. The body stretches downwards to the left with two curved strokes suggesting back legs, and a scribbly patch for the tail. The formless splotches cannot be explained. Lori made no comment, only declared firmly that her picture was a "Lion."

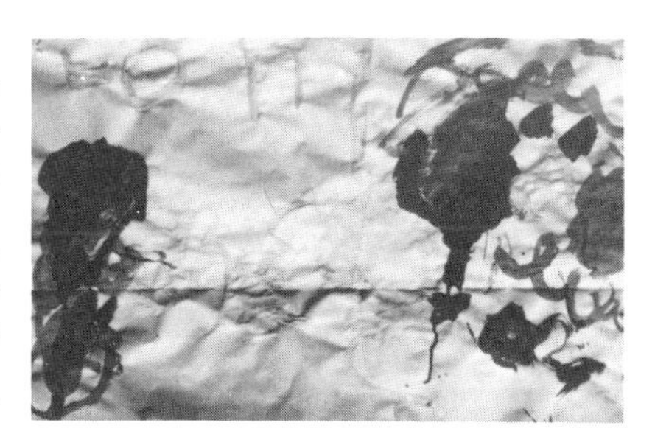

or fingers. Engrossed in his activity, the child may talk and illuminate his intentions to a certain extent. Like Lori or Rochelle, he may give his scribbles a title that indicates what he had in mind, but which the adult cannot see in the scribble. However, children who work silently and do not give any clue to what they intend likewise have ideas and feelings that urge expression.

To see examples of the scribble-shape development by Trenton and Lori, view MEDIAPAK 4, frames 1-25.

(A) Children start to scribble at different ages and continue this activity for different lengths of time. Rhoda Kellogg's studies are outstanding for the enormous volume and variety of scribbles she recorded. She demonstrated almost countless different kinds of beginnings and developments. However, informative as the thousands of collected examples are, rarely do they relate a particular kind to an individual child and his personality through sequence or change. Each child's scribbles differ from those of another. Children also vary in the length of time during which each maintains certain characteristics before entering another period in which his "style" of scribble changes. John, Trenton, Valerie, Carma, and Lori had very individual and quite different ways of scribbling. Indeed, Carma's scribbles are a fitting illustration for the origin of the word scribble, which is derived from the Latin word "scribere"—to write. She herself described her scribbles as "writing" and identified with this in making hand motions of writing. So did Valerie. The movement, the sen-

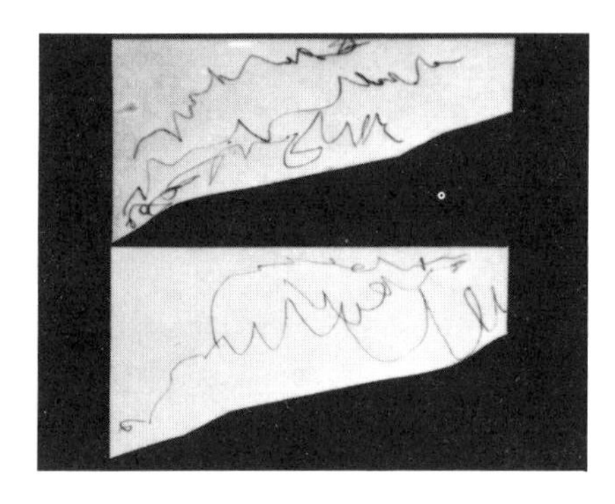

At two years, five months, Carma declared these markings to be "Writing." Her scribbles were now becoming interlaced and complex.

sation of the hand motion, is as intimately connected with her scribbles as her image of writing that she hoped to emulate. The scribble technique is used at a more advanced art level for drawing curly hair or for picturing smoke from a chimney or a train engine. Dense scribbled lines are also used to show there is something "inside," such as a person's stomach.

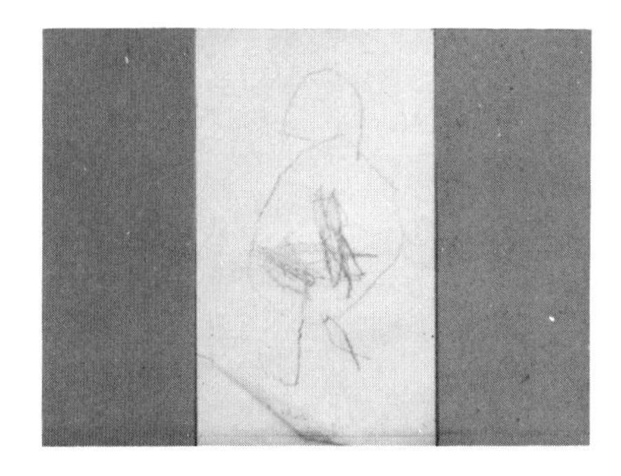

Scribbles also may indicate something that is "inside" or that can be "felt" inside. Julie scribbled a patch inside her very primitive figure of a "Lady," probably to indicate the "guts" or what she "feels" inside when she is hungry or has a stomach ache.

Older children sometimes return to scribble to express an experience which they cannot describe with their acquired picture-signs. Claude, who at ages three and four already had a remarkable aesthetic ability in his visual expression, turned back to scribble when he wanted to picture musical experiences.

For examples of individual children's scribbles and shapes, particularly by Carma, Maya, and Valerie, view MEDIAPAK 4, frames 26-55.

(B) Joining the ends of a line seems to come about by mere chance. When a child becomes aware that a shape has been formed by a closed line, he may name it, as John did, who called his first shape "dog," or Valerie who pronounced hers a "boat." There is a period, usually quite short, during which the child mixes scribbles and shapes but does not lose sight of the discovered shape formation. Now, he goes on making them with purpose. Their variety leads him to see resemblances to animals or objects and later on to people. He may associate the shapes with activities like running or flying. He may discover, perhaps by association with a memory image or because of a detail in the shape he drew, that what he made *is* an image of something. Once his shapes do not just happen but have a vague resemblance to something real, the child strengthens his shape in this direction. Then he makes it more definite by remaking it many times. Ultimately, even the outsider may see a likeness. The *shape phase* has been considered part of the unrecognizable scribble period. For shapes (and scribbles), mass data have been assembled and then put into categories by type and form: round, square, ladderlike, spiderlike, etc. However, these statistical findings only give information on the variety of forms and perhaps percentages of their occurrence related to age levels. They do not clarify which specific shapes (or scribbles) any one child creates and adheres to, for how long, or how he develops drawings of given shapes in his sequences.

Interpretations of the beginnings of children's picture making prior to the schema are highly speculative. Various assumptions have been put forward for why they draw and paint at these early ages. One such theory sees in the first scribbles or splotches of paint a manifestation of the

At age two, Rochelle experimented with blue chalk, seeing the imprints its edges leave on the paper.

child's "self," his ego. Any mark on paper or other material is a sign for a self-assertive communication meaningful to the child. Whatever scribble or shape the child pictures on the blank page is an expression, a communication of *his* ideas, *his* feelings, *his* world, a non-verbal meaningful pronouncement. Shapes and scribbles are "figures set against a void."

The empty part or the void of the child's drawing space is described as the ground against which scribble, shape, or figure stand out. The emptiness around and between his lines and paints, the ground of the paper, represent a distant, as yet unknown outside that does not touch his life yet; therefore, *for him it is a void.*

The very young child's random dots, hesitant strokes, and shapeless forms, though generally similar in character, show individual differences from child to child. Each child maintains and develops his own difference,

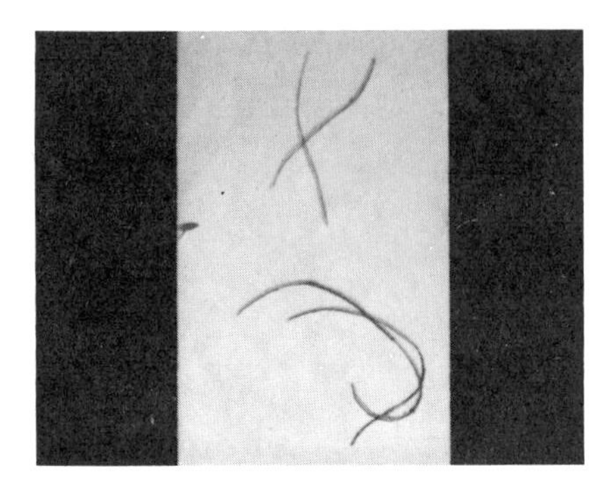

In her first two scribbles, made at twenty-two months, Norena was timidly but deliberately finding out what she could do with color on paper.

comparable to a personal style of handwriting within the general form of writing used in a culture.

The activity of making scribbles and shapes is not simply a visual activity. It involves the urge to move and the coordination of movements. The child's urge to express experiences, thoughts, and feelings leave a record of them through his marks on paper — this is his non-verbal way of speaking out. All these factors spur his efforts to explore his abilities. Though they are incomprehensible to others, the making of even these primitive forms gives him satisfaction. His complete involvement in this complex activity is an important aspect of development. How can we determine to what extent a single factor, or several, activate the child? How can we explain an art activity like Catharine's? Between the ages of two and four, she named some of them and left others unexplained. Some of them are aesthetically superior, amazingly technically perfect and sophisticated in line and color. These surely held a promise of future art to come? Yet, by the time she reached kindergarten and grade school, the bloom was off, her child "art" was over.

For examples of shapes by Kim, Rochelle, and Joanna, view MEDIAPAK 4, frames 56-75.

(C) The age when scribbles become shapes also varies individually. Some children spend months, even years, making shapes. Trenton did this. Others continue their shape drawings while developing recognizable schemata of people, animals, and objects. Lori's shape phase lasted many months. During this time she continued her scribbles but also developed man-figures and objects. Thus, for a time, Lori's art work covered three phases simultaneously, a vivid example that a child who attains the level of a more advanced representation does not necessarily or consequently drop her previous stage.

Rochelle who for a few months did mostly large area-paintings (as did her sister Joanna two years later), also made brush drawings, to many of which she gave titles that clearly described what she had to say. Without her titles, even a wild guess cannot catch the meaning of her pictures. In some of them she translated sensations of an entirely nonvisual nature like her "Bumpy Street" into literal visual form. Kim, who shows another example of the mystery of shapes, was prompted by quite definite intentions that she pursued assiduously. She enlightened her puzzled mother with her titles. A rare example of steplike development is Norena's "Fish."

For examples of transition from shapes to emerging schemata by Norena, John, and Anne, view MEDIAPAK 4, frames 76-90.

(D) Generally, we can state that the viewer of shape-phase pictures cannot find any resemblance to the real thing the child indicates by title

Julie's line technique in this labyrinthian aggregate made at four years, three months, is very complex. The drawing looks like a fantastic compilation of toys.

or comment. However, with the child's help, we can interpret the meaning of some lines or paint forms, and may find similar shapes in other children's pictures, which may lead us to understand other children's intentions at this stage.

The child often does not give any directionality to shapes, even to partly recognizable shapes and emerging figures. He turns the paper while picturing to suit his convenience. However, there is no up-down or above-below that tells the baffled viewer how to hold the paper while looking at it. The young artist seems to have dropped single shapes on the page at random, as Benjamin did in numerous drawings. His shape drawings require careful scrutiny to find the tiny, tucked-in-between schemata that he had perfected. There usually is a relationship between the shapes strewn haphazardly over the page or in tight and complex shapes (aggregates like John's or Julie's), but it is almost impossible to figure it out—just as it is difficult to unscramble the meaning of a group of words without a verb and no apparent logical sequence.

There is little doubt that the children discussed here were incited by their life experiences to work them out in pictures. Their scribbles and shapes, impenetrable as they seem, are the starting point of future understandable communication. Even in these early beginnings, the characteristics of their similarities, and the individual ways in which children develop them, may be helpful to adults in observing differences among children and understanding individual developments. We can recognize that all children take the same direction, that their initial drawings can be described as scribbles and shapes, yet that every child has his own particular way, his own special "style."

Module Six

Emergence of Figures and Objects:

At some point in their early development, children begin to picture living things and objects in a recognizable manner. Their drawings and paintings *emerge* from mere shapes or scribbles when the child adds some identifiable characteristic. He may add some detail or change part of the shape

Although David's first "man" at two years, seven months was a line scribble in a helicopter, it was followed within days by a "Man" with body and legs.

and thus transform his pictorial image—giving it a resemblance to "man" or "object." Not only is he now able to identify his creation himself, but the outside viewer also may be able to do so. Not only does man emerge, but animals, plants, and objects do also.

When and how do children arrive at picturing their figures and objects in a recognizable manner? Generally they do so between ages three and six. Age levels at onset of emergence from shapes vary as does the duration of the process of emergence and its subsequent preschematic development. The degree of development may be no more than a barely recognizable shape or it can be definitely recognizable.

The differences in the quantity of art that children produce seem to be related to the duration of their shape period and the time of emergence

Emergence of Man

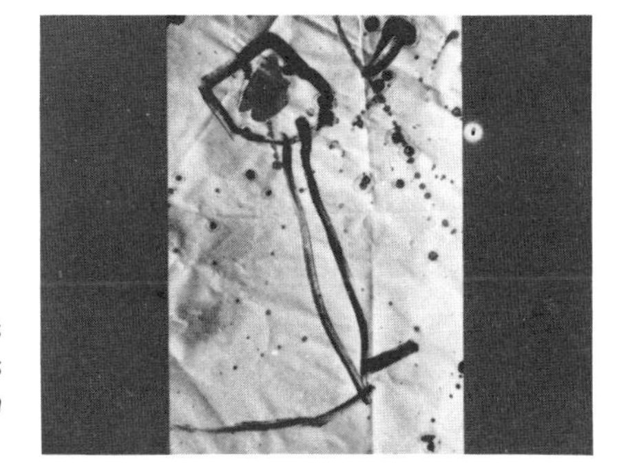

Different from others, three-year-old Catharine's first man drawing is distinctive for its long legs and feet, while its face is only a contour with a blob inside and two color dots for eyes.

from it. Some of the children in this program, observed through long periods, made very large numbers of pictures, others few. Some of them did a relatively large number in a single day. Some did their picturing continuously; others had spurts of activity. However, the quality and maturity of the figures and objects children draw may not be too different. Quality and maturity cannot be judged by a single piece of a child's art. Many drawings or paintings are needed for knowing about a child.

During the child's early years, picturing may be only one outlet among many. For some children, noise may be a favorite and necessary outlet of feelings. They shout, sing, play with pots and pans or instruments like drums and trumpets, or experiment repetitiously with the sound of words. For others, action is imperative. Some combine action with noise-making. Then, it may be gesturing in the form of make-believe acting, or it may be dancing or strenuous motion like tricycling, racing, and running. But *there are children for whom picturing is the favorite activity, perhaps the most meaningful of all.*

When children draw, they are often vicariously representing their experiences. Every child, at a very early age, has some strong interest that dominates *what* he draws and *how* he draws it, whether that interest is people, or motion, or touch, or other experiences of their senses. Perhaps because the child's love for his family and his dependence on it is so important to him, he communicates this feeling-complex by trying to *draw people first.* The moment he draws something supposed to be "man," which the parent can recognize as a man, the child experiences a shock of delight and is satisfied with his success. This same feeling may also be experienced by the mother and father who can now see meaning in their child's picture making. After this, the parents may keep their young one's work. Unfortunately, many pictures that follow this first man are judged no good and are thrown out. The "good" ones are recognized as landmarks of advancement and growing skill. There seldom is an opportunity to study what happens in between unless, as shown in this program, parents cooperate by keeping every bit of the child's output over many months or years. In rare instances, parents have done that all along on their own.

Maria's mother, for instance, kept her daughter's first "man," but two years elapsed before she began collecting Maria's entire art work. This happens frequently. After the great interest in the first man-figure, time passes before the child begins to develop a variety of recognizable subjects. Then parents once again pay attention and appreciate the value of their child's pictures.

While the child works towards his emergence of figures and objects from mere shapes, he may continue to draw or paint as he did before. Anne, in her compositions of many objects, drew recognizable figures, but also put in the same pictures many unidentifiable shapes. The meaning of the picture, therefore, remains obscure to the adults despite their recognition of part of it.

The man-figure, judging from statistical studies, is the most interesting result of development from shapes. This is not always the case as you can see in David's, Benjamin's, Claude's, and even Catharine's emergence pictures.

For examples of first man-figures, view MEDIA-PAK 5, frames 1-27.

(A) Usually, the child's first man-figure is only a head-man. To the head he may add two lines for legs and sometimes two short lines for arms. But the head alone, all by itself, can stand for the man-figure concept. *There is no body.* As Ricci pointed out in 1886: a head, two legs to go for a walk, what more is needed? The head is the most detailed part of the drawing and usually the largest. It may stand for members of the

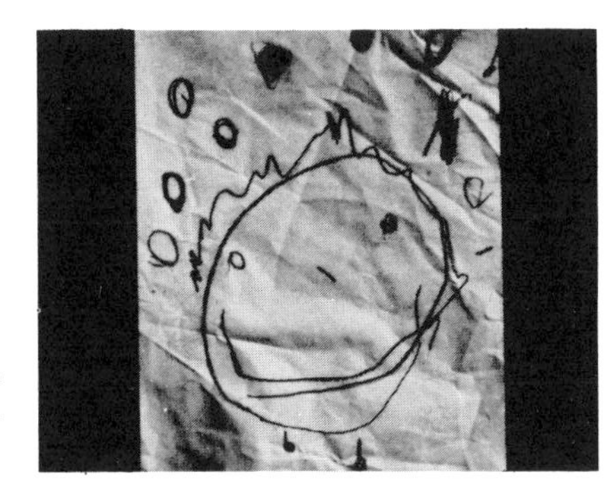

Lori's drawing here is essentially a head, made at three years, eight months, with mere indications for the two miniature legs.

child's family, as in Lori's "Window Play," but also may portray any person important in the child's life. It also may be a self-portrait. Erin first drew herself.

Erin also shows interesting features in her two drawings. "Brother Mark," at left, was made at two years, eight months. In the middle is "This is Me," a self-portrait made at age three. At the right is another "Me," a primitive schema that she made at four years, six months. She is holding a bottle with, perhaps, some insects.

Man-figures look alike in structure but differ in their general appearance, in peculiar details and techniques, according to their creator. Differentiation is achieved by size, attributes, number of parts of the body,

In "Two Brothers in the Park," Kim depicted a scene with fence, sun, and what may be a bird in the sky. These drawings were made at the same age at which she struggled with painting houses and trees unsuccessfully, but was successful with animal pictures.

and other characteristics. For a time, each child's individually shaped figure remains almost the same, repeated again and again. It stands for his idea of "man." For the child it embodies a concept, an essence of his Self. It does not necessarily appear so to others.

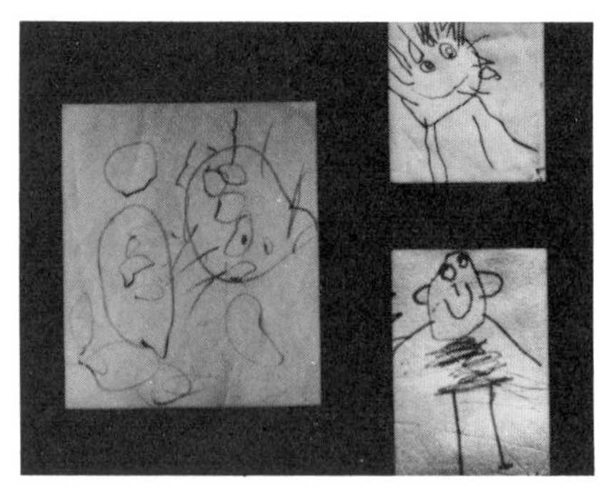

The face at left made by Carma when she was two years, six months old has two eyes and lines for the mouth. It was evolved amidst similar, but meaningless, line shapes. In some of her other drawings (at right), Carma shows initial emergence characteristics: a group of shapes at left at two years, six months, and two tiny figures at right at three years, four months and ten months.

Maya's man-figure emerged at age two years, ten months. She developed it during the next nine months, first adding details to the face, then a body, and finally clothes. However, after having developed it to some extent, Maya retained the same structure and style for later figures in her developmental series. This interesting series is long and can be followed step by step. Halfway through the series, her concept of figure

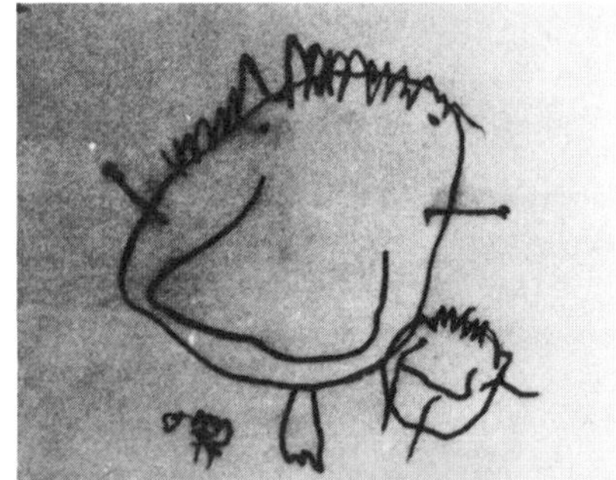

Maya's first man, top left, at two years, ten months is the beginning of a long developmental series. Maya developed her emerging man-figure from age two years, ten months on. The figure shown top right is a group of three called "Mother and Children." The four figures shown at left, still head-men, were drawn by Maya between three years, four months, and three years, six months.

had stabilized and, even after the final drawing had been made, she used it for large numbers of later pictures without much noticeable change. She stayed on a plateau, that is, her development did not actively progress for a while. Plateau situations occur in many children's developments, sometimes several times. Maya used her figure drawings like puppets that enact various roles in different situations. Details or props clarify the situation or story content. Later, Maya pictured her mother, herself, her sister, and others with increasing elaboration of details relevant to feminine appearance or to the story she tried to picture.

Already in the second of her man-figure series, she made a group in which she showed how "grown-up" her mother appeared to her and how small she considered herself in relation to her mother. But in relation to her younger sister Carma, Maya drew herself very large, even larger than she had drawn her mother compared to herself. Between Maya's painted and her drawn figures or objects, there is a distinct lag in picture development. Maya was well aware that a variety of details and enrichments for story telling purposes is better shown through drawing. She also developed objects such as houses, cars, pieces of furniture, and even street lamps.

Rarely does the emergence of the human figure or other schemas directly follow the scribble stage. However, Becky's emergence of the man-figure did follow her scribbling without a shape stage, and the same happened with Valerie.

Valerie, two years and two months old, struggled almost desperately to draw people. At first attempts, she drew what seemed to be long-stemmed flowers. She called their blossoms "men." Her mother showed her how to make a schematic human but, of course, Valerie was unable to copy it.

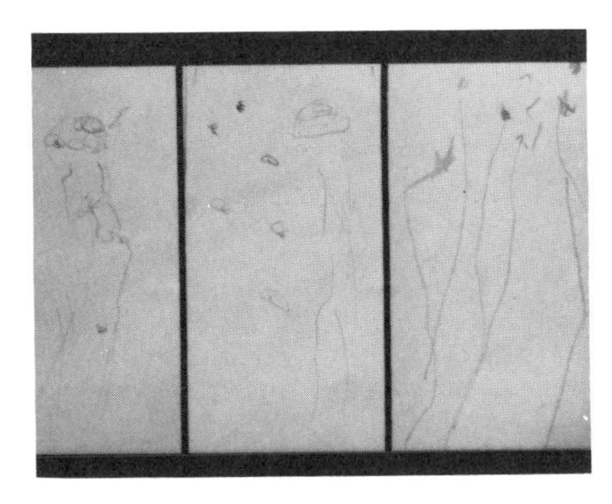

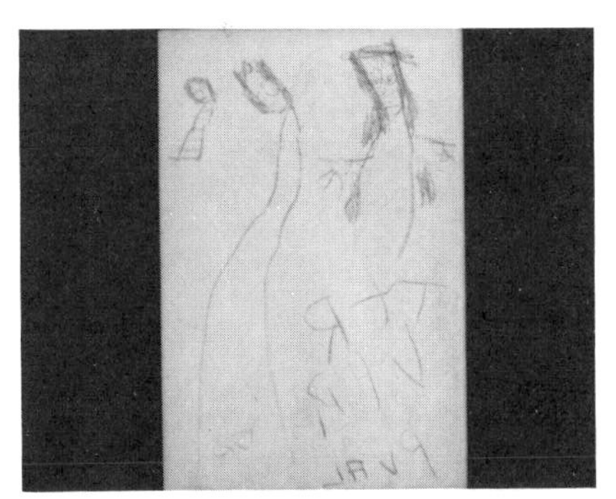

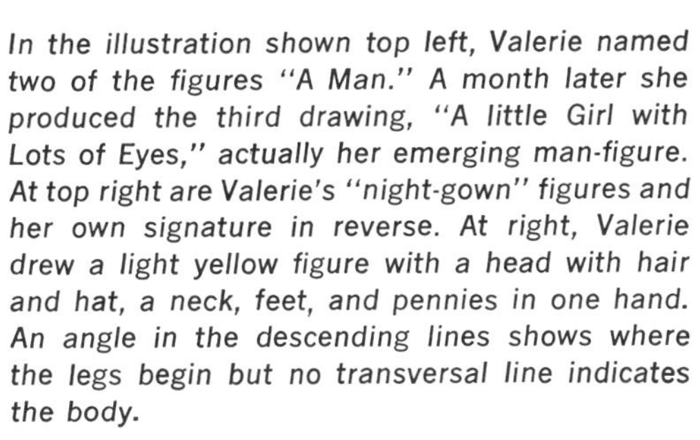

In the illustration shown top left, Valerie named two of the figures "A Man." A month later she produced the third drawing, "A little Girl with Lots of Eyes," actually her emerging man-figure. At top right are Valerie's "night-gown" figures and her own signature in reverse. At right, Valerie drew a light yellow figure with a head with hair and hat, a neck, feet, and pennies in one hand. An angle in the descending lines shows where the legs begin but no transversal line indicates the body.

Yet her mother's sympathy acted as a stimulant. Valerie's series from emergence to primitive human schema was very different from Maya's. The evolution of her man-figure was of an unusually individual character.

For additional examples of early man-figures, view MEDIAPAK 5, frames 28-55.

(B) In contrast to Valerie's difficult and laborious trials in picturing man, Trenton's "man" emerged after a very long stage of shapes and came quite suddenly, like a flash—Eureka! A Man! Not only did Trenton exclaim excitedly over his sudden and complete achievement, but his mother seemed as excited as he was. Trenton continued at once at a furious pace, and on the same day made twenty-two man-figures. The first of these was called his "best" of the day. It may be that sometimes a first creation is the result of particularly close and concentrated attention, while following pieces are done faster—too fast. In Kim's series of house shapes, her first one was also the best. Continued repetitions appear to be a necessary activity for every young child. They usually seem to be efforts at further improvement. By trying over and over, the child seems to make sure of his skill, gain confidence in his ability, and also enjoy the comfortable feeling of growing more familiar with his subject. However, repetition may become automatic, and sometimes temporary deterioration sets in. Trenton simultaneously developed long sequences of houses, animals, and scenes of nature.

Anne's emergence of man-figures was different from the usual development. On the one hand she proceeded from a lumpish shape to head-contour and face; on the other hand, she used the contour of a leaf as a

Anne had an unusual source leading her to her faces. A Christmas tree in leaf form with a stem, rounds for ornaments on its edge and inside, led her to a few inside rounds and a short line and then to a face inside the Christmas tree leaf.

setting for a human face. She might have intended it to be a flower, but she also drew it as a "Christmas Tree" with ornaments. The two derivations existed for a time side by side, interchangeable: man-face and tree-face.

John, Anne's younger brother, gradually made the translation from shape to man. Shortly after succeeding, he changed the style of this emergence and proceeded with a primitive line schema.

In his transition from emergence to primitive schema, John applied heavy paints for his "Guitar Player" at age four.

The *emergence of animals* follows a course like that of people. Animal heads are seldom made in profile at the start; they usually are made similar to those of people and frequently have human faces. An additional detail, like whiskers or pointed ears characterize them at first as animals. Unlike the head-man, the animal energes with a body, quite similar to the body given at a later point to man. The animal body usually is an oval or squarish shape and, contrary to man's, is laid out horizontally, with legs hanging from its underside. First, there may be many legs, later only four. Some children may develop a profile head at this initial stage in their effort to create an essential animal likeness. Trenton did this. It is fairly usual that differences between emerging man-figures and animal-figures are difficult to recognize without the child's own identification. Jill's animals and people so resembled one another that her pictures of her mother were not too different from those she made of bear or elephant.

For examples of emerging figures and primitive schemata by John, Carma, Jill, and others, view MEDIAPAK 5, frames 56-94.

(C) The emergence of plants is not as readily noticeable as that of people and animals. Plants seem to be drawn as schemata from the very start. The first appearance of a fir tree, with its simple vertical crossed by horizontals, is well illustrated by Catharine's picture in MEDIAPAK 2. Kim's awkward attempt in her shape paintings is a distinct emergence from shape to tree. Color splashes seem to be the principal departure from mere shapes toward recognizable flowers. Their arrangement gives a flower effect that becomes increasingly defined in the following paintings. Julie, Catharine, Rochelle, and Lori all drew and painted flowers. Details, color, and one or two characteristic lines make them recognizable.

David and Benjamin are examples of the surprising fact that the emergence of objects can take precedence over the man-figure or other living things and that these objects continue to be the subject of a rapid development. However, all children make a few pictures of machines like airplanes, cars and trucks, trains, and the like.

Whether the man-figure or animals or objects of their surroundings emerge first in children's drawings depends on a child's primary interests, like Allan's "Deepsea Diver" or David's "Helicopter." Furthermore, several of the children, during their phase of emerging figures and objects, almost simultaneously pictured their surroundings. These were compositional arrangements or scenes around their early man-, animal-, or object-schemata. The duration of the emergence seems to be related to the child's concentration on a single item like man, to the child's repetitive exercises in improving his efforts, to his individual observations, and the information he acquires. Secondary interests evolve later in children's drawings or sometimes appear suddenly at a later date and in a more advanced stage than that of emergence. For David and Benjamin, man was secondary to objects. For Catharine, trees were of particular interest; for Kim, animals. All these variations reflect the individual personalities of young children. Once the child's pictures emerge, the adult who carefully studies the drawings and paintings is better able to recognize a child's particular individualism. In fact, he may follow what the child says through them, even when no titles or comments are offered.

Module Seven

The Schema:

Maya's foremost interest was people. Once she had developed her primitive schema of the human figure, she used it with few changes for innumerable drawings and paintings. It seemed to her sufficient for communicating such events as the birth of her sister in a story of thirty drawings.

In accordance with the importance of what she wished to tell in her pictures, Maya developed her schemata further, added details, or created new schemata. If the action in a story called for a long arm to reach an object, she lengthened it to adjust to its required function. If only *one* arm was needed, she drew only *one arm for the doing.* To underline its

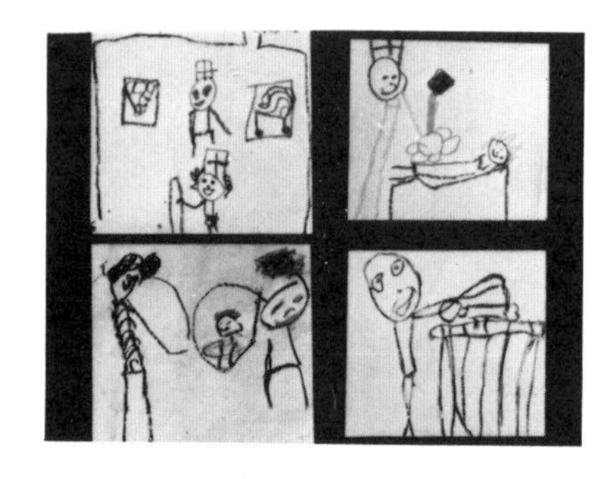

Maya shows here the hospital where sister Carma was born (top left). With her huge hand, the nurse gives "Medicine" to Maya's mother (top right). The "Nurse is giving Carma to Mommy" who receives the baby with encircling arms (bottom left). At home, with his long arms, "Daddy changes Maya-Baby" lying on a high table.

activity, she fitted it out with a giant hand, like a baseball mitt, to show clearly the object it held, medicine or diaper. Other children use similar ways for their picture language.

Maya's earlier pictures resemble one another like members of a family. Hence, a baby looks like a replica of her other human schemas, but laid out horizontally. Object schemata were likewise characterized: a baby crib looks like a cage on long, vertical legs; a bike is recognizable by its wheels, spokes, and handlebars; a car schema is a simple square on wheels, its driver another specimen of the human schema adjusted to a sitting position. Maya made clear the function of each figure by some important detail, like an over-sized nurse's cap with a cross on it or a long stethoscope dangling from a man's neck. Maya gradually added attributes that made her schemata less primitive and more complete. She paid attention to the appearance of people and their clothes, as when she drew "Cinderella."

Maya's visualization depended much on color. This showed not only in her preference for painting, but also in some of her drawings that she treated in a "painterly" manner, like her "Church Interior" or "Airport." She also liked to *draw with brushes.* The width of her brush line was substantial and its sweep gave body to her figures and objects—a very different effect from scribbly, scraggly, drawn lines. Painted contours, filled-in areas or bodies, the width of even a single stroke for leg or

Maya seemed to follow an irregular pattern in development. At age five, she made a schematic drawing of herself and sister Carma (who again is tiny). During the same summer, she painted in yellows and browns a "Lady with big Hat" (at right), well proportioned and so "painterly" that it strikes the viewer as realistic.

arm, all conveyed a three-dimensional feeling of bulk. Indeed, these pictures resembled "expressionist-impressionist" attempts at painting. Maya's style of painted schemata became perfected toward the end of her fifth year, as in her "Lady." Her paintings show that absorption in color may, in a way, dictate shape and style of a schema.

Maya's painted schemata were economic. Similar to her drawings and those of other children, her distinguishing attributes told what was happening but, contrary to drawing, the various features and details were indistinct and less understandable. Maya, at four, drew and painted groups of people and objects. She made compositions dealing with events, stories, or situations, but she also painted simplified schemata of things that symbolized experiences, like her birthday.

Different from Maya, Anne's figure drawings were soon past primitive schematic representation. When she portrayed "Ernie," her father, her schema has progressed in several aspects: proportion, flexibility, and the individual characteristics of her model. Anne's development, shown at its best in "Ernie," was rapid. People's faces acquired individualized features; positions of the figure, like that of "Ernie" in a sitting position,

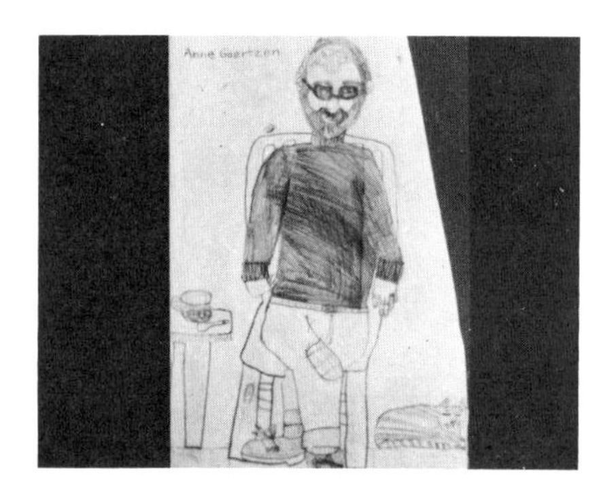

Anne pursued her studies from live models like this "Portrait of Daddy, Sitting." Eight years old, she drew him with his cat at his left, a cup and spoon on a table at his right, and a tiny butterfly perched on the back of his chair.

appeared natural and flexible and were quite clear. In spite of some realistic features, her more complete and enriched drawings remained schematic in style and still continued to be so at age ten. Anne drew many compositions, groups of people in two's or three's, like her "Dancers" or "Bathers," but also larger numbers of people such as her school

When Anne entered first grade, she made many friends and put them all in a picture, all schematic yet individualized.

friends. She positioned them mostly in rows, aligning them on a groundline that she either drew or indicated by a substitute such as grass. Sometimes she added a flower or a bug. Such a little addition of a thing of nature made them more alive.

When Anne presented a subject requiring the picturing of space, she not only did it by alignment, but also combined front- and side-views or bird's-eye-views, a combination characteristic of schematic representation.

Some children acquire a large *pictorial vocabulary* of schemata. This is rather typical of the complete schematic stage. They work out many details for their single figures and objects. Each child selects what he is most interested in, regards as most necessary, and then refines his drawing accordingly. This is his way of showing what is important to him, what is on his mind. Though quite aware of the actual proportions,

Becky's schemata at age four and one-half are still primitive in parts, like this pen drawing of "Lady with No Clothes On." It presents a "smiling" face and a none-too-complimentary picture of her body.

he may not use correct proportions among the parts of a single object. Even when he is able to do so, he may use incorrect proportions among single items in a multi-figured or multi-objects arrangement that constitutes an entity. He may give an insect the size of a child, or a flower the height of a house. A child's schema does not correspond to reality in the adult sense of proportions or space illusions. When complete, his

Ananda at age four and one-half succeeded in making a happily "Dancing Princess," with facial features and limbs at the right places. A frog is present with a crown next to it. Ananda cut out her picture, probably to be used as a prop for playing.

schema still does not make use of this kind of knowledge. He may put in decorations, embellishing details, and in this manner create an attractive piece of "art." Action and movement are indicated by slanted lines or sinuous fluidity. The child explains in his developed schematic style quite clearly all he wants to make known by the positions of his figures and objects and by emphasizing the center of interest of what he is presenting.

Within a complex schematic composition, the development of single objects or living things may be unequal. Some figure, man or animal, may be fully drawn as a developed schema; others may be still primitive and have insufficient resemblance for adult identification. Such a mixture rarely bothers the child. More advanced development of humans does not necessarily mean that he will also bring other things proportionately to the same level of development. Lori may be mentioned as the prime example for using scribbles, shapes, and primitive schemata simultaneously within the same period of art activity. She abandoned that in kindergarten under the teacher's guidance. Only when a child enters the intermediate state of schematic and realistic representation does he seem to become conscious of these disparities.

During his schematic period of representation, the child tends to repeat his particular subject matter, figures, places, and objects over and over.

This unusual, patterned organization of car motif by Anne at age five may be due to a playful repetition, but it also may be Anne's version of a traffic jam at rush hour.

Apparently, these repetitions strengthen what he has found out, has learned, and help to build his Self. He is using picture language as he does spoken language.

The child seldom changes the fundamental schema of the figure or object he has developed. He makes alterations, "corrects" proportions, adds details or other attributes, but keeps essentially the same schemata (as the word indicates). The schema of one child, though a schema, has a personalized appearance. It remains different from that of another child.

Few of the children were under observation at age five, six, and on, the age when they leave the primitive schema behind and use their developed complete schema. Maria, Kate, and Cheri only joined in the study at the age of five. Full schemata, therefore, are a lesser part of that period in child art here discussed. However, there are some children whose achievements are in-between, like Naomi, Ananda, Becky Ann, and Jennifer. And there are a few children (Anne, Becky, and Benjamin) who participated long enough in the study to reach a fully developed schema.

Outstanding among Naomi's schematic pictures is her portrait of her younger sister Julie. It is remarkable because this particular portrait in

"Claude's First Classroom" is truly schematic. The details that interested him are shown in a curious space and size representation that showed what he thought important. We see the teacher, a small figure in profile, in her chair, a table with a bowl of white fish in front of her. In the foreground is a very large fish tank in front view with goldfish and a water plant. No children, no other equipment.

pen and colored inks portrays the essential babyishness of a seventeen-months-old child. In some story pictures, Naomi also had gone beyond incorrect proportions and had been able to make space drawings that were complex but clear.

Ananda, another child with primitive schematic figures, made swift progress toward a complete schema through an interesting maneuver of learning. Her brother Allan, her mother, and Ananda played at drawing a figure, each of them in turn drawing one of its parts. Ananda was helped, apparently, to overcome the primitive state of her figure schema by observing the devices her brother Allan used, without losing her own "style" of drawing.

For examples of the schema of childhood art, view Maya's 30 drawings and others, MEDIA-PAK 6, frames 1-36.

(A) Allan's schemata were different from other children's shown in this program. Because he dealt mainly with ghosts and scary creatures, he was concerned with inhuman faces. By the time he reached age six, and because of his multi-figured fantastic scenes, he perfected his schemata of people and animals by keeping their sizes small. Once past the primitive level of his schemata, he was able to give his small humans and animals fair proportions. Most of Allan's compositions dealt with his fantasy world and were peopled by large crowds placed in large spaces among isolated trees or in an interplanetary vacuum. Like other children, Allan constantly repeated his individualized schemata.

While the drawing by most brothers and sisters differ greatly from one another, as did those of Lori and Trenton, the drawing of younger siblings may be influenced by an older one. The abstracts of her outstandingly talented brother, many years older than she, fascinated five-year-old Becky Ann. Real abstracts are strange to a child of her age, nor could she have copied them. But she invented abstract-like patterns in her

Although Becky Ann, at age five, did many pictures similar to schemata of other children, she was strongly impressed by her older, talented brother. She tried to imitate his ornamental abstracts as shown in this richly decorated schematic figure with elaborate ornamental lettering around it.

brother's style to cover the dresses of her figures and drew similar single decorative motifs. However, she also made her own lively schemata, complete in their way and showing motion.

Jennifer drew her primitive schematic figures with fine, almost elegant line technique and continued in this manner while developing her schemata. Hers was a gradual process. Her drawings make it difficult to

Jennifer drew this sophisticated "Chinese Lady Singing," (left), which she infused with a "Chinese"-like appearance. Six months before, she had drawn "My Grandmother Dancing" (top right). Both drawings were small and in fine lines. The tiny pen drawing (below) of the "Baby in her Crib with Mobile" shows Jennifer's ability to make many details and object schemata at four years, nine months.

separate the primitive schema from the development of the complete schema. All of Jennifer's drawings showed a style in her schemata that set them off from those of others discussed here. She added simple surroundings to her figures, also created compositions, a complex undertaking always surprising in any preschooler.

Many children undertook to unite many items into a single picture. This has seldom been recognized or reported for these early ages. Usually, it is associated with later periods of development as a developmental step after the complete schema has been achieved.

At age five and even later, many of Lori's figure drawings still were primitive schemata. The kindergarten environment brought about a change toward more complete schemata. However, the compositions she made at home showed a dramatic and advanced ability in portraying nature and people in nature surroundings. They were vivid and showed movement and action. Yet, they were populated mostly by primitive schemata.

Development of the schema is usually gradual, seldom sudden, but sometimes it can be rapid. Maria, five years old, at first drew the heads of people very large in proportion to their bodies. Her figures already were drawn as complete schemata, but still looked stiff. They often were enriched with details and embellishments like the dress in "Mother and

Maria, whose art work differs from others in this group at her age level, shows schemata already developed and complete. Maria's "Farm," drawn at age five, shows her schematic characteristics and her exuberance and humor. She contoured each figure and object, aligning people and animals in front views. She made a bird's-eye view of the garden behind and added one "realistic" dog in profile and another with a frontal human face.

Children." Her compositions were balanced, often near-symmetrical or centered in a definite way to point at what she thought most important. We might speculate whether Maria started to group her figures and objects long before she was five because toward the end of her sixth year her compositions were already rich and complex, as shown in her twelve Christmas pictures.

All Maria's schemata, until age six and one-half, show similar characteristics. Compared to her drawings of people, some of her animal drawings were developed, some almost close to realism. Her animal schemata still were disproportionate in scenes with people or other animals and plants. Insects could be as large as mammals, birds as large as some figures,

Interested in insects, Maria made a series of "Bee" pictures. Here, a bear, licking his chops in anticipation of the honey contained in the tree he faces, is pursued by a swarm of bees. The tree is simplified, the bear mostly recognizable because of the situation, but the bees are shown in detail.

as in her bee series. Maria made well-developed schemata of objects: see-through houses filled with furniture, cars with people, and others all full of life and humor. Maria's plant schemata, when they occur at all, are incidental but also well developed.

Until the age of seven, her schemata of people, animals, and objects barely changed in character, but at age seven other trends appeared, some constructive, some destructive in terms of art development. Her verbal facility as well as her ability to write had advanced greatly; therefore, she sometimes added dialogues spoken by her picture people in her complex compositions. Maria developed a new economic line technique that was interesting, and she did it with taste and understanding. On the other hand, her speed in drawing increased and with it she showed negligence, even sloppiness, in execution.

For examples of developed schemata and grouping by various children, view MEDIAPAK 6, frames 37-69.

(B) Kate had passed the age of emergence toward the schema, gone through the development from primitive to complete schema as seen earlier in the horse-and-rider series, and moved on to her specialty, houses. In the "Sierra Cabins," we can observe the development of enrichment in a basically complete schema. Kate also drew a variety of other schemata, portraits, flowers, trees, masks, and valentines, and birds and insects, all of which, because of her individualized technique, can be singled out as her "art."

David's schemata stand out among others because of his almost total concentration on representing the world of machines and transportation. He developed specific schemata for them with particular attention to improvements such as structure of parts, their properties, and refinement in representation of these items. Therefore, from age four on, his schemata became complete. Yet, some primitiveness in their appearance persisted, due largely to carelessness of execution. He created surroundings for his cars, trains, and trucks and provided a schematic perspective of the space in which they moved. He made distinctions between his single objects by slightly altering some attribute. He drew trees and other plants rarely but, when he did, they were clearly developed as were his few figures.

The various objects in David's compositions sometimes were scattered, more often tightly packed together. Where necessary, he used a groundline or, if he wanted to indicate separate planes, he added more groundlines from fore- to background. He sometimes made a maplike arrangement with front- or side-views of houses or people along the roadside; these attempts, however, were sporadic and abortive. Only his compositions of war, fire, exploding rockets, and the like were so arranged as to make an extraordinary impact.

Children of preschool age, up to age seven or later, cannot copy with any reasonable or efficient results. Their drawings spring from memory, the outcome of internalized images. Many parents believe that copying is a sign of talent, even when it is poor and lifeless. Very young children almost never try on their own to copy or, if they do, they recognize the futility of their undertaking. By the time children are nine years old or even older, they may be able to copy or imitate the technique of adult representation. David did so when, at seven, his interest turned to science and he wished to make illustrations of scientific subjects.

Cheri, with her exceptional ability and almost telescoped development, is unique among our thirty children. Her development was described in Module Four and her pictures served as illustrations for the entire range of changing general characteristics from schema to adult drawing.

The development and eventual elaboration of schematic drawings and paintings that represent humans and other living things, habitations, transportation, and machinery is determined by children's differently oriented and specifically centered interests. Among the children here discussed, the very young furnish examples of processes in art development. These developments differ chronologically and in matters of elaboration, richness, and kind. *Few children at this very young age attain fully developed schemata.* Here, all children, in their schematic pictures, showed abundantly their outer and inner life experiences, the knowledge they acquired on their own, the impact on their senses, their perceptions and their feelings. Once in school, few continued with their home art activities; almost all showed the limitations they experienced through the curricular art in school and their own submission to being directed.

Module Eight

Line and

LINE AND CONTOUR, A STRUCTURAL FACTOR

Lines and contours seem to encourage the child in developing and emphasizing structural characteristics. These are of great importance to his pictorial development, and more than any other mode of drawing, contribute to the development from unidentifiable shapes to recognizable forms.

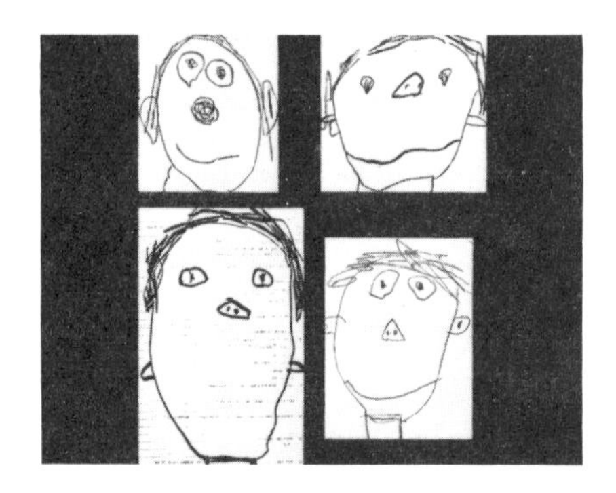

Trenton, at four years, two months, drew three of his "First Man" series partly with crayon and partly with feltpen. He did not care with what he drew nor what the lines looked like. The head at right bottom was drawn in finer lines nine months later and is almost identical with the first of his earlier series.

The observer can follow the steps in development of contour-lined shapes which tend to clarify a shape until it becomes recognizable.

Norena outlined several longish oval shapes, making each one slightly narrower than the one before. Then she added, perhaps accidentally, a dot at one end. This must have helped her internal image, and the finlike additions she drew at the other end then strengthened the image of "fish." Carma, not a prolific picture maker, drew a number of contour-lined shapes that led eventually to human face and figure. As with most very young "artists," the steplike sequences were achieved with lines. Sometimes children develop the overall character of the object, but more often they outline one or more details which help identify the intended object. Without these details, the main shape would remain a puzzle.

Most children find pen, pencil, or other pointed tools best to picture clearly the structural characteristics of real things in their surroundings: man-figures, animals, plants, objects, or machinery. Children do not erase. They seem to feel certain of every line. Pen and ink best demonstrate that the child relies on his internal image. If they consider their drawing "wrong," they throw it away or leave their failure and may strike it out.

Children who try to paint contours with brushes rarely are able to show any details with accuracy. They continue with color and paints because they enjoy working with them, but manipulate their brushes as if they were pencils or crayons. Paints are not as easy to control as pointed tools are. They are less serviceable in defining objects recognizably. Paints are enjoyable to use, give interesting effects, but frequently delay development of form. The child who paints appears to remain for a longer period in the phase of unidentifiable shapes or primitive schemata than if he were

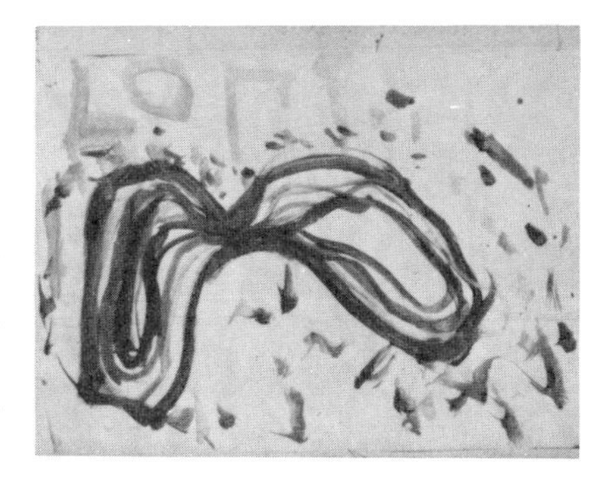

Lori's drawing in paints of "A Long Snake" at four years, nine months aims at two characteristics: first, the length of the snake, its width presented by the width of the brush stroke, and second, the contortions of the snake movement, which she could follow with the brush most easily.

using a tool better suited to advance a development strongly dependent on outline. Therefore, generally speaking, children do their *recognizable painted objects at a later date than their recognizable line-drawn pieces.*

Kim's paintings of animals give the impression of an earlier phase of development than her drawings of animals. Her painting technique hindered the necessary contour forms. Rochelle, preoccupied with paints, was unsuccessful when she attempted to paint contoured figures, but more successful in using pen and ink or pencil. Once aware of this fact, she drew recognizable people on anything at hand—even a crinkled napkin. Lori made many linear figures on small pieces of paper, even entire scenes. At the same time, she continued shape painting in large numbers. When she tried to paint figures, she could only poorly trace their contours or indicate what they represented. Her paintings quite definitely lagged behind her drawings of figures in development.

Erin did not seem to make pictorial gains when drawing with crayons because she made ragged contours. Her pen technique in lines was more controlled. Jill's pictures are instructive when we compare her drawings with her paintings. Her work showed significant difference in developmental achievement with the two media for similar subjects during the same month, sometimes during the same day. David's pictures are based entirely on contour lines. He was most interested in representing the structural aspects of objects. He wanted to show their function and, for this end, line technique was the logical way. He drew hastily, made dense and

David's fantastic "House-Truck" with his family, made at four years, three months, is an aggregate of partitions, inside and outside, and the separate vehicles passing it. It is a labyrinth of pencil lines showing the structure, functions, and innumerable details of all parts.

jagged lines, unconcerned with a "good" appearance of his art, and his compositions are often confusing. He wanted to get on with what he had to say. Later, when the nature of his drawings became more and more descriptively illustrative (but also lost their liveliness), David learned to draw more minutely and to use clean lines.

The rate with which a child develops in drawing ability is highly individual. There is no reason to hurry development. However, when a child is eager to represent specific forms, he may become disappointed, even feel thwarted by medium and tool. Many children discussed in this program were given a variety of media at one time or another and encouraged to use them. They were curious and responded. Usually, after trying a different medium once or more often, the children returned to their own favored tools and techniques. Their curiosity in media seemed quickly to be satisfied unless the new medium served some definite aim of the child's picture communication. This was the case in Claude's and Paul's use of blow technique.

For examples of line as structural contour, view MEDIAPAK 7, frames 1-27.

LINE AND STROKE—A FORM FACTOR

(A) During the incipient stages leading to recognizable forms, line contours are particularly helpful. The emergence of figures and objects and development of primitive schemata depend mainly on line. Lines serve the child's need to clarify the form in which he can express his inner images and help in due course to fully develop and enlarge his pictorial vocabulary.

Careful study of many children's work during an extended length of time shows that each child has his own *character* of line. Its quality may change, but the child retains something that distinguishes even his scribbles at almost any time from those of another child. One child may apply lines with strength and decision; another may set them down very delicately. Some children place their lines densely and cover a small area completely; others make few lines widely apart so that much of the ground remains visible.

Children differ not only in the manner they trace their lines but in the actual character of the lines themselves. Their form and direction may differ. Some children make straight lines and go back and forth in the same direction. Lori made these kinds of lines. Some children make rounds, spirals, perhaps starting at one side of the paper and ending at the opposite edge. Carma's scribbles were of this kind. Others make their lines in circles, as if pirouetting around an invisible center. John tended to scribble in this manner.

Most scribble lines seem to be continuous. They often are difficult to disentangle and follow through, and their beginning and end may be difficult to find. It is as if the child's fingers pursued an activity without cessation or interruption. Benjamin's lines were drawn in this manner. A very young child seldom draws a long straight line from one side of the page to the other, or lifts his pencil continuously to make very short lines. Mostly, the children in this study made continuing lines.

Sometimes children's early line techniques give the impression of the lines being made with intensity and speed. Sometimes lines appear to be made with deliberation, as if the child were intent on creating a particular pictorial effect or sign. One hesitates to describe this variety in a general sense. Even when very young children talk while scribbling or making shapes, we cannot be certain whether they are explaining their line scribble or shape pictures or merely making comments at random. Sometimes their intent is clear. However, in the period of shapes, especially when on the verge of qualifying the meaning by some explanatory line addition, the child's explanation may clarify what he has in mind. Further elaboration of line combinations tend toward a recognizable form, as can be seen in many of Benjamin's drawings. Sometimes, in developing primitive schemata that seem odd and yet can be recognized as a figure, a child provides an explanation of the oddity, as Becky did with her "refrigerator-football-grandma" changes. In instances of this kind, the child is unable to pursue his first aim, but sees that the form he created has more than one meaning. He can, therefore, change his ultimate goal by adding some "telling line" as a characteristic.

Each child seems to have his own distinctive way of using lines for contours and details. In drawing, the different colors of the lines do not seem to influence their line-character. However, when the lines are painted,

Maria drew a "Peacock" in profile with plumage spread (at left). Using feltpens, she characterized the decorative form of the bird and his stance far more vividly with her line strokes than with a brush. Contrary to the economy of line in "Ernie," Anne, at six years, ten months, drew (at right) all kinds of line fantasies when she interpreted the personnages of her stories.

there is a strong difference in their role and the results that are achieved. Maya had a distinct line technique that she maintained in her thirty drawings of the "Birth of Carma" and most other drawings. Similarly, Lori used her line technique throughout with some modifications in her drawings. However, both children, when they "drew" with paint brushes, used techniques very different from those they used in their drawings. The two children also differed from one another in their lines, whether drawn or painted.

Allan's lines, when drawing his favorite topics, ghosts or haunted houses or other "unreal" subjects, were tremulous, as if he were shivering when drawing these subjects, as if transmitting through his lines the scary, yet delicious shudders that he associated with his visions. However, his lines for "real" things were firm, even heavy.

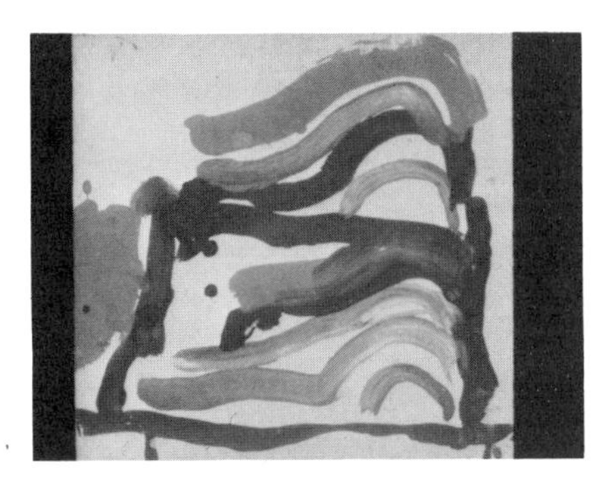

In Maya's sensory experience, a bed like this "Doubledecker Bed" (at left) and its coverings are something one feels. At four years, two months, she represented its shape in sideview and its bounce with thick, curved paint strokes. A wide black brush stroke (at right), seemingly made in one sweep, was Maria's way of characterizing Snoopy, the beloved hero of the comics.

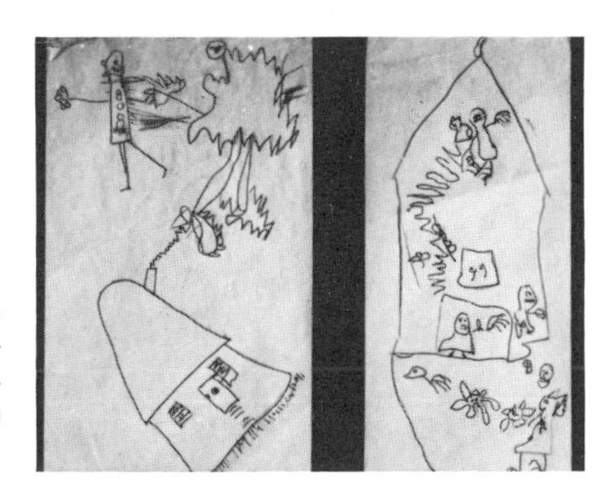

In Allan's "Man Running Fast from Ghost to His House" and another "Haunted House" (at right), drawn six months later, the zig-zagging, purposefully unsteady lines are stronger still. Other children sometimes use such lines when they draw witches.

Anne is an exception among the children of this group. At age four, when already drawing figures and compositions, she amused herself with occasional fantastic line convolutions. In her sixth year, she developed a genuine understanding of the visual value of line, of its peculiar merit of expressiveness in pictures. She used lines for structural purposes but was also able to use them to translate other intentions. Furthermore, she calculated the value of line as a contrast to watercolor. But she also drew story characters with costumes elaborated by complex line configurations.

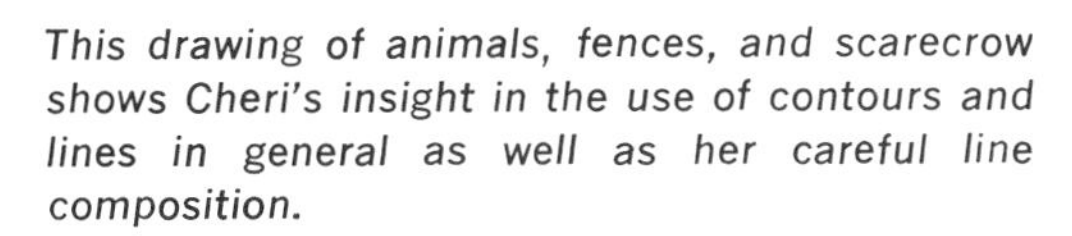

This drawing of animals, fences, and scarecrow shows Cheri's insight in the use of contours and lines in general as well as her careful line composition.

Cheri used lines *consciously as an instrument of expression*. Her use of line was economic, to the point. With a few strokes, she gave importance to a contour, clarified a detail, or characterized the elusive nature of motion in her animals. She established her drawings as "pure" line drawings.

Maria, Kate, and Anne achieved their own individual differences in their use of line at a point when their schemata had emerged and become complete.

It is instructive to observe how much individuality very young children achieve with line and stroke, but it would be a mistake to believe that this can be taught by rules and methods at these young age levels. Insight into each child's use of line and its character may help a child to strengthen his own incipient technique, but the variety and potential of growth even in this respect is a challenge to any adult's understanding and guidance.

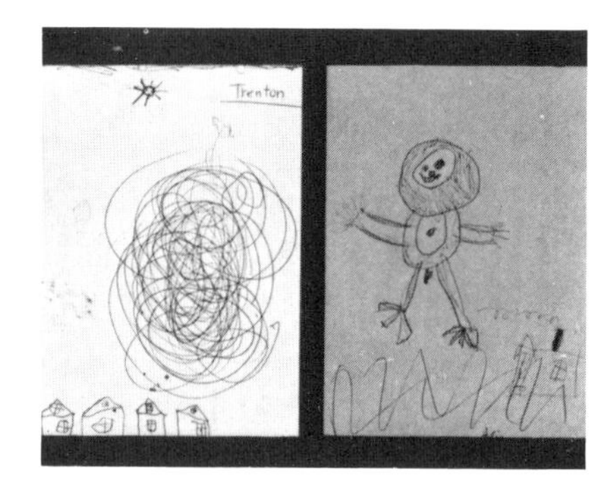

Trenton, nearly five, here made a delicate line drawing in color pens, evoking the light feeling of "Clouds and Sky." The "Boy" next to it by Julie, four years, two months, is also drawn with light fine lines. Dashed on the paper with a writing pen, the boy seems to be jumping.

LINE AND COLOR INTERACTION

Line drawings are not necessarily monochromatic, or made with pencil or black ink. Young children mostly draw in colors, whether crayons, color pencils, or feltpens. The color serves as contrast. It adds body and substance to contours. It also may be a counter-balancing element to the linear structure or command attention for some detail.

Kate embellished her theme in "Sierra House at Christmas Time" with many details, all done with fine lines and pointillist color dabs of her pen. The rich line technique is basic to the fairylike quality she created.

In early development, very young children like to try out a number of colors for their lines; some select carefully and purposefully only a few colors that may reflect their concepts and infer some special, personal meaning. Some children use color as an addition to their lines, a contrast that may emphasize the pattern of their lines and make details or "new" parts conspicuous. On a very early developmental level, color differentiation may point to differentiation of parts, figures, and objects. Becky used color for this purpose, and Jennifer did so occasionally. Some children use color as an element of form. These children may attain aesthetic results, as did Claude or Paul or Anne, or Catharine in her earliest years.

A color drawing, however, remains essentially a drawing, different in impact from a color painting. It combines the developmental advantages of

Maria's "Flower-Fairy," drawn at age five, shows color line drawing at its best.

lines for structure, form, and details with the more sophisticated results of a stroke technique and, very important, permits a child to indulge his love of colors.

For examples of line as form factor and color, view MEDIAPAK 7, frames 28-49.

Module Nine

Color is an important factor in children's picturing. The very young approach it as something delightful and meaningful. In fact, until they are about five, they usually see color as a substance in itself, not as a mere attribute of things.

The child observes color in clothes and in the hair and eyes of playmates and family members. He admires color in animals and knows every detail of their coloring: eyes, paws, fur, wings. Most of all he enjoys the blue of sky and water, the colors of flowers, birds, and insects. At an early age he finds color a source of attraction, pleasure, and wonder.

Children explore color very early, even when they scribble, and make use of it in an individual manner. When a child begins to make shapes and to develop the man-figure, his treatment of color becomes very personal.

There are children who use color only incidentally and say what they have to say through lines and shapes. Some forget about color after doing only part of a picture and continue in only one color. David was inclined to do this. It strikes the viewer of David's drawings that perhaps the effort of coloring may have hindered his urgency to speedily communicate a wealth of ideas. There are also children who find one particular color more suitable or attractive than multicolors or black. When the drawing itself is the main interest, a single color may be quite sufficient. Many of the drawings by Rochelle, Benjamin, or Maria were in a favored single color, especially red.

Most very young children favor a range of colors of their own, even choose a single favorite color for a given period of time. They may remain in their "red," "green," or "blue" period for some months. They may use even the same tool during this period.

Color

For many children, color may be the most satisfying means of expression. They may use color almost like a sign language—different colors to show something new or important—very much as they draw certain parts disproportionately large or exaggerate characteristics of significance.

Maya was fascinated by color. A face could be a color blob, indeed the entire picture could owe its meaning to color. Even her early scribbles were mostly in paint. She wielded her brushes with flexibility and, by twisting them, took advantage of their width. Her early painted schemata show that in many ways she manipulated her brushes as if they were large, square-cut color feltpens. Whatever she could express about figures and objects with color and motion seemed to satisfy her. Her color imagination could overcome the handicap of working with crayons so that she created quite sophisticated combinations. For Maya, color was a language, almost self-sufficient.

Lori also had a strong preference for color, which showed as early as her paint scribbles. During this period, she even had specific color combinations such as yellows and greens and experimented with mixtures of this kind. She continued this during her painted shapes period, while drawing vivid primitive figures. Painted figures then lagged behind. Only when Lori reached age five and one-half did she master painted schematic figures. Unfortunately, her use of clear, strong colors and her free brush strokes seemed to vanish with this attainment.

Color can play several roles in pictorial communication. Favorite colors can project a meaning. Generally, meaning and importance differ for each child and these differences show in their paintings. Children often use color to express sensory experiences that have nothing to do with sight or actual color. They may use color to convey joy, love, or exultation. They may employ color as a vehicle to show moods created by star-gazing or by festive or scary occasions. Such graphic expressions are beyond understanding of most adults despite their empathy with the child's experiences.

Some children use color crayons and color feltpens for "drawing" or for "painting." If crayon or color pencil strokes are mixed, the results are often dull and the texture crude unless used with infinite patience and some experience with the effects of mixing. Feltpens can be superimposed on each other and still retain their vivid colors unless applied in too many layers. It is also possible to make smooth, yet varied lines with them. Some children superimpose their color strokes to achieve new color mixtures. Others set strokes of various colors closely together with crayons or pencils, thus giving the effect of a "new" color. Anne and Joanne used this technique.

In using paints, children find out early that strong colors, when mixed, may become dark and murky. Some discover that they must choose carefully if they want to achieve vividness or delicacy of color. Rochelle used colors with extraordinary vividness when, at age four and one-half, she painted "Water and Land" in heavy layers of color. Shortly after, she made a series of flower paintings, the last of which was a triumph of sheer color over form. On the day following the Fourth-of-July fireworks, she expressed her impressions of this memorable occasion in a variety of "designs" in color. Her younger sister Joanna also was able to convey, by colors only, what she wanted to say, as we saw in MEDIAPAK 2.

Curiosity, a spirit of exploration, and inventiveness spur the child on within the limits of his individual direction and development. Results of his experimentation may be both startling and satisfying.

Some children proceed with boldness in their paintings, using brushes dripping with paints. They execute their ideas swiftly, often forcefully. Others like Catharine, handle their paints delicately and deliberately, measuring the amount on their brushes to avoid dripping, manipulating them carefully as if they were fragile. A few children at an early age seem to be able to work with a wide range of watercolors, a very unpredictable medium. Benjamin tried them successfully, and so did Anne with continuing excellence. In all cases, the child must find out how to relate paint to paper or whatever material he is using. Claude and Paul sometimes achieved startling results.

The material itself may be important to the child. During the scribble stage and shape period, one child may feel that the paper should show and not be made to disappear under a mass of colors, while another regards the paper only as a necessary surface for the paint and may cover the entire ground area.

When given a choice of colored papers, very young children sometimes pick a favorite color, then paint on it with the same color. They may use yellow on yellow, green on green, or all kinds of dark colors on dark grounds, indifferent to the relationship between color and ground and the fact that the paint does not show up against the background. It would almost appear that they are satisfied with the "doing" and have little concern for the outcome. Or perhaps they do sense the situation when they see the results, but do not see any need for contrast or know how to achieve it.

The tools with which color is applied are various. Color pencils, crayons, and feltpens are color and tool in one. For paints there are fingers and brushes. A variety in width and softness of brushes permits a variety of effects. There are other techniques. Interesting effects can be gotten by blowing through straws on little pools of paints spilled on paper. The results of this technique are mostly accidental, indeed they are surprises, and young children like surprises. However, if a child knows what he wants to achieve, he can blow in a planned direction and control the speed as well as the amount of color he distributes; he also can improve the results with a brush. Kindergarten students often are shown this technique but exercise it haphazardly. Claude and Paul excelled in achieving their own ends this way. Other kinds of effects can be obtained by applying paint or ink on one half of a page, then folding the paper over. The result is a symmetrical color figure, shapeless, or perhaps vaguely resembling an animal. Some children get striking results, although these, too, usually are accidental.

Square or round pieces of sponge dipped in color offer another way of working with colors. So is the use of a dropper, dribbling paints to achieve the desired shapes. Some children use a combination of these techniques with success. A talented child with imagination in technique may plan his results and use the paperground as one of the color factors. Claude and Paul experimented repeatedly in many paintings.

There are children who have become immersed in color and painting and want to continue in this medium. Those children who love painting try to develop their figures or objects with paint and brush and find that these are not suitable for progress in development of new schemata. Usually, their efforts disappoint them because they need more precise contours and characterizing details. Many of them then abandon their attempts and continue painting for the sake of colors, producing unidentifiable shapes, blobs, and areas. Their figure development is delayed. Others, like Maya and Lori, make parallel attempts in painting and drawing and find a pointed tool more rewarding for some specific purposes. Eventually, they also produce figures in paint technique but on a less developed level than the one attained with pencil or pen.

Observation of individual children during a satisfying length of time shows that children who particularly love colors and paints carry on in other media that present an opportunity for color use and color enjoyment. Rather than to renounce color, they try to find materials that are favorable for expression in color and develop techniques that satisfy these needs.

For examples of the use of color in children's art, view MEDIAPAK 7, frames 50-87.

Part Four

Art Histories of Four Children

Module Ten

The Picture

Benjamin was, at first, a very quiet child. Around his home were trees and birds. Trucks and cars passed on the divided road in front, but there was no dense traffic. He spent time outdoors, sitting under a tree, watching, sometimes in company of a neighbor child. His parent's house was small, simple, and snug, a comfortable place for a young child. The family had a dog who, though "accepted," stayed mostly outdoors and did not seem part of the child's indoor world.

Benjamin's father was then a commercial artist, and drawing and painting were, therefore, familiar activities in the home. What was more natural than Benjamin also trying to make marks? When he was twenty-two months old, his mother began to keep his early scribbles, which were already

This is the first picture Benjamin's mother kept. The scribble, made with purple and green feltpens in strong and fine lines, is interspersed with shapes. The long, intertwined, complex lines cannot be the first that Benjamin made on paper.

interspersed with shapes. Among examples saved from this period nothing points to "first" pictures, though he may have made some tracings in sand or dust before his mother provided him with paper, crayons, feltpens, pencil, and pen. She encouraged him and showed her interest by keeping his drawings.

Biography of Benjamin

At age two, Benjamin drew shapes, small rounds so tightly filled with spirals that they looked like tiny balls of yarn. Open lines meander around and between them. These lines are not scribbles in the sense of being haphazard and jumbled. On the contrary, they appear to be drawn with

Benjamin here drew "Train-engine, Boats, Bulldozer with Man," a shape aggregate that dominates the page in size and complexity. The boat is a shape with a spirited smokeline just above the rear of the engine, cutting in a slant toward the left. Turning the page by ninety degrees, we see the bulldozer in the left upper corner, its shaft protruding, the man's head above the edge of the cab.

care, apparently with purpose. Sometimes the balls are in a chainlike series, sometimes they touch one another. Ball-like shapes frequently appeared in Benjamin's drawings at this time, surrounded and intersected by lines that seem to pursue complex paths.

When Benjamin was twenty-six months old, he often drew three short lines forming a rectangle with an open side, sometimes with a fourth line closing the rectangle. Some of these he subdivided by lines; on others, he made one single line longer and protruding. Benjamin called these "Flags." He also drew aggregates of shapes, each consisting of a rectangle topped by another one, with squarish wheels underneath and perhaps rounds on top. These he called "Trains, Flags." One of these pages of drawings called "Trains, Flags, Ladder" has a tiny regular engine tucked among the shapes, and a still tinier ladder like a diminutive lattice. Benjamin crowded as many of these shapes and objects on a single page as he could find space to fill.

Benjamin's interest soon also turned to boats. At first the boat shapes were difficult to recognize, but soon he made them more distinctly and drew them with assured lines. He placed them among the cars and trains. One could detect an object resembling a train engine with a window and a scribble inside it to indicate the engineer. In all these drawings, Benjamin seemed concerned with his shapes and objects as single entities.

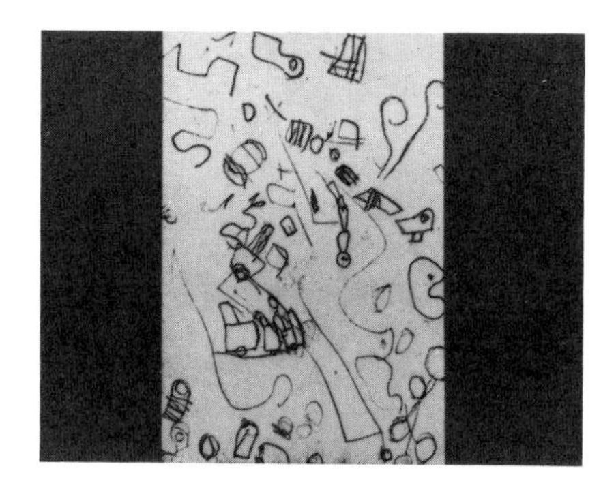

At two years, four months old, Benjamin included "Boys" with the many shapes that he drew on each paper. To see the "boy" (center), one must hold the drawing in one direction; to see fish, or train, or balloons, one must turn the drawing.

They show no interrelation, nor any relation to the page. For Benjamin the page was nothing but a ground on which to make pictures. He turned the sheet of paper around with no regard to direction, probably in search of any space for one more little picture.

Benjamin soon made very distinct and sometimes larger-sized "Boats in the Water" with wavy lines below to indicate the water. Birds also appeared at this time in his drawings, some fairly large, surrounded by a great number of unidentifiable shapes or "boats." In his many small drawings, fish as well as birds became recognizable because of their body shapes and eyes.

Benjamin's titles, if any, were laconic. His mother explained that, until two or three months before the author met him, he had not been given to much talking, nor to profferring explanations or comments concerning his pictures except by single words. Shapes which are difficult to identify must, therefore, be given the benefit of the doubt. Benjamin may have had a definite intention not explicit in his picture but which expressed his thought or feeling.

Benjamin, at two and one-half years, was still fascinated by trains. He added airplanes and helicopters to his subjects, probably stimulated by flights he saw when visiting his grandparents. He also continued to put birds in his pictures. Later he added campers and houses and house-trailers. He "manned" his machines with pilot and driver or passenger, visible through and within his structures. This strange effect is very like the transparent houses made by many children up to age nine or ten, or the people in "see-through" boats and trains first observed by Corrado Ricci in children's drawings of the mid-eighties of the last century.

In his third year, Benjamin made some detailed fine-point drawings such as his "Fire Engine" or "Fire Engine Boat." In these and others, he lavished increasing care on perfection of details of certain single objects among the boats, trains, cars, and tracks in his drawings.

At the threshold of age three, Benjamin occasionally volunteered more enlightening titles: "Rocketships with Propellers and Lots of Windows Crashing into a Car." This was an action picture soon followed by others such as his "Roller Coaster." Action pictures often need two or more objects between which a relationship either is apparent or assumed. Benjamin started to draw fewer pieces on a page, three or four instead of his prior multitude of objects. He even made a single object on his drawing paper, such as one "Boat" with two funnels and portholes with people's faces.

DRAWING DEVELOPMENT

Benjamin's development in pictorial representation began as early as Becky's, at just under two years of age. His choice of subjects was distinctly different from that of Becky, Claude, Anne, and other very young children. His favorite subjects were machines. Only two living creatures, bird and fish, appeared frequently during the first months of his drawing activity. When he reached age three, he paid some attention to his man-figure, but in his world of machine objects, man seemed necessary only as a mere supplement to the machine.

Benjamin's object development was rapid and his progress fairly continuous. In early drawings, unidentifiable shapes surrounded recognizable objects, giving the impression that, in repeating such shapes, he may have searched for better ways to express what he wanted to show. Sometimes it comes as a surprise to find on a single page one well-developed car or engine among many meaningless shapes.

For examples of Benjamin's early drawing development, view MEDIAPAK 8, frames 1-29.

(A) He drew with great speed and amazing assurance. The author observed Benjamin's drawing activity when he was two years, eleven months old. He changed from pencil to pen and ink and back again while he drew with lightening speed ten objects on three pages, among them a "streamlined" train, the first such he had pictured.

When Benjamin was three years, eight months old, his family moved to Canada. Judging from his drawings, his travel experiences had a great impact on him, broadening his interests and outlook. He continued to represent all kinds of transportation but now enlivened them with people. His roads, as if seen on a map, were flanked by "schematic" cars, silos, and other buildings. He even made lighthouses, particularly interesting since Benjamin was far from the ocean. Baseball players and high-rise buildings appear in his pictures as well as buffaloes and camels. He made drawings of mountain trips, frequently with trains, tunnels, cars and trucks, airplanes, and cable cars. His drawings seemed to be a combination of the reality he saw and his own fantasy stemming from stories and things he had learned in his Canadian nursery school. During this time, Benjamin signed his name in distinct block letters. His great desire to write was discouraged in his school, but he signed his home drawings.

Trains

Benjamin's development of his favorite subject, trains, can be followed from box-shape to box-on-rollers, to engine, to a sequence of train cars, and to train tracks. But the course this development took was not as logical as it sounds, nor was the advance visible from one drawing to the next. The train engine, for example, appeared once when Benjamin was twenty-six months old, an astounding compilation of complex shapes, but nevertheless a locomotive. It reappeared in simpler structure, yet more characteristic in shape, at twenty-eight months. Benjamin had meanwhile developed his train cars further, though they still lacked windows. Soon, he assembled several of them to form an entire train. He

At two years, five months, Benjamin drew the train cars set next to one another, but not together. Here, a trainman is perched on one of the cars. Lines indicate the tracks. Every unit of these three trains on tracks is distinctly separate and going in a different direction. There is no spatial relation among them.

then proceeded to make train-track combines and added windows to the trains. At age two years, eleven months, he pictured the fluid movement of a modern train.

Figures

Between age two years, four months and three years, three months, Benjamin progressed in his figure representations from a man-figure with head, body, and legs to figures with arms, hands, and fingers.

At two years, four months, Benjamin produced a figure that was fairly large compared to his other diminutive shapes. This, according to his mother's comment, was his first man-figure. It had a round head, two eyes (one of which could be a nose since it is on the head contour), a body like a longish box, and two legs. Through the next months he made few figures. In a drawing named "Boy, Fish, Trains" and some others like it, the figure of the boy is hard to recognize although the fish, boats, and trains are plainly identifiable. However, he did not always form the entire body, but sometimes only made head and legs. At one time he would show details—at another time he ignored them. At first, Benjamin's figure treatment seemed to depend on the importance assigned to the figure in relation to the machine subject of the picture.

In one of his early pencil drawings, made when he was two years, five months old, he made the figure of a trainman, a head with some details, legs and feet, "attached" to a car. The figure also could have been interpreted as a humanized bulldozer with a teethlike shovel. In another drawing of three trains, there is a figure which perhaps was meant to be a passenger. This figure has a head, two arms emerging from mid-head, and two legs, and appears to be suspended over a car. This is not unusual. Many young children, even at ages six or seven, when making a horse and rider, separate the rider from the horse as if he were suspended above it. A similar suspension can be seen in Paul's "Christ on the Cross," in which Christ is drawn separately above the cross. In airplane drawings of the thirties, the pilot was shown astride or above his plane.

Benjamin, at two years, eleven months, made some single man-figures, their arms, with hands and fingers, stretched from the body; there was also a curious horse with humanized face. In one pen drawing, he portrayed himself in a striped shirt with his "Daddy" and "Mommy." This was significant insofar as he had not attempted to picture his family before this time. Now he drew more people, some of them leg-men. Like the oversized head of a head-man who has tiny legs and usually no body, the leg-man has a very small head, but very long legs. Some of Benjamin's figures had bodies. He also now made people looking out of houses that he made with doors, windows, and smoke-belching chimneys. He drew "Grandma's House" and her family.

Benjamin continued to picture people more and more frequently. For instance, he put his family and bystanders next to a house. One of his

The crowd of children around the giant leg-man with an umbrella (or could it be Gulliver surrounded by Lilliputians?) is drawn in red crayon, testimony to Benjamin's interest in people at three years, ten months.

pictures, drawn with visible speed, shows in the center a longish figure with an umbrella surrounded by innumerable people, probably children. He drew sun and clouds, showed the ground by a line, but made no plant.

For examples of Benjamin's trains and figures, view MEDIAPAK 8, frames 30-51.

Representation of Space

(B) An interesting aspect of Benjamin's early drawings had been the multitude of single shapes and objects crowded on a single sheet of paper. It seemed as if, in a quite haphazard manner, he scattered cars, engines, parts of trains, and "just shapes" all over the page while turning it round and round. Although Benjamin returned at times to this manner of using the space of his drawing page, he started to evolve short but distinct baselines for small groups, usually trains. At first, the arrangement of a series of cars suggested an invisible baseline. He soon made a line across the wheels or at their base that indicated tracks. Next, a baseline appeared for single vehicles, car or even boat, as an indication of position or direction. Benjamin's train drawings, usually two or more on the same sheet of paper, showed a separate baseline for each train. These clearly differentiated the separate trains as entities and the direction in which each moved. Benjamin had arrived at the well-known "alignment," although he applied it for a while in a restricted manner.

One particularly confusing drawing was made by Benjamin at age two years, four months. It showed that, despite a variety of spatial positions and directions, he may have followed an underlying unifying concept. At

A study of this drawing, made at two years, four months, by Benjamin, shows four views around its center. They appear to form a squarish frame if looked at from above. In the view shown here, we see waves and a docklike base for ships and boats, while the shape in the center may be a helicopter. Turned ninety degrees, the figure reveals two more baselines with train cars and, close to the center, a line across with wheeled shapes. A figure stands upside-down, probably showing that the man is on the other side of the track.

first, this drawing seems to only present a number of sideviews of boats and trains. Upon inspection, we discover a central shape around which various side views appear to form a squarish frame. As in a bird's-eye view, this square seems to represent four points of the compass. After careful study of the very involved arrangement, we cannot help but assume that the entire page was not done at random but was a composition intended to represent a harbor. Unfortunately, no comment was made by the child which might have confirmed the spatial interpretation of this most fascinating, untitled picture.

At this point, Benjamin seldom resorted to drawing many nonconnected subjects on a single page. He made fewer pieces on one single drawing paper and no longer presented them in different directions. Now the viewer could find the positions of single objects clearly defined as "up" and "down." During his fourth year and from then on, he made use of the well-known method of alignment in children's space representation. He placed the main person or object centrally and drew a base- groundline along which everyone and everything was aligned. Empty space above indicated the air, a sun above or clouds indicated the sky at the top, or in later drawings of undersea subjects, he placed divers, fish, or other sea creatures below the groundline.

For examples of Benjamin's use of space, view MEDIAPAK 8, frames 52-69.

Transition

(C) Benjamin entered a period of transition when he moved to Canada. His interest still was strongly involved with machine objects and transportation. While traveling, he observed cars, trucks, swishing by on the roads, trains passing, and train yards. He also added space capsules and rockets to his already varied machine vocabulary. Fast-moving things fascinated him and he drew them in long, looped lines and scribbled loops suggestive of speed. The people he saw, in houses, in campers, or on excursions into mountains; the objects characteristic of the plains, such as silos or haytrucks; scenes from the mountains, with peaks, and precipices, trees, cabins, and mountain climbers, all of these were digested and became part of his understanding of the outside world through drawing them. For his drawings he now had to develop many different schemas. We can follow this process and the progress he made.

As he added new subjects, Benjamin changed the size of paper and his use of paper space. He changed his manner of drawing lines and of placing people and objects. He became more interested in people and colors. For instance, he made a single figure in blue and purple lines with two enormous fingers holding a red umbrella. He became interested in colors. Except for early color crayon scribbles and a quick sequence of eight painted patches in vivid colors, he had been content with pen and pencil.

Now he tried watercolors and handled the medium with lightness and a feeling for the transparency peculiar to water colors. No sketching outlines seemed necessary. Benjamin used brush and watery paints as directly and with the same assurance that had been so amazing in his early pen and inks.

SCHEMATA AND TECHNIQUES

As time went on, Benjamin's capability increased in picturing the wealth of his observations and fantasies. The stay of his family in Canada had widened his world: awareness of the outdoors, of nature, of life on the plains and in the mountains. Different from many of the other children here observed, Benjamin did not picture an abundance of flowers and trees, of birds and insects. He was moved by the larger aspects of nature,

Benjamin made this complex pen drawing in which he placed various ships on the sea and planes in the air and filled the ocean with many creatures. Three divers (one in a capsule at lower left) are exploring, while a man is being drawn into the jaws of a fearful fish.

not the solitude of nature, but man's invasion of it and his inventive ways of reaching it and getting around in it. His subject interest still remained close to man's machine world, but he related it to the wonders of nature that he had experienced and that he remembered, a year later, when his family again moved, this time to flat midwestern country. His pictorial narratives were crowded with all he had seen in the past, what he had felt, had projected himself into, and identified with. They make us aware of the intense, vivid, inner life that was Benjamin's up to the last pictures seen during this study, when he had reached the age of six and one-half.

Occasionally, because of his widened awareness, Benjamin pictured campers with people in them; houses in danger of fire, but fire engines on hand to rescue them; the big city with its skyscrapers and overloaded telephone poles; life on and below the water; home life; the joys of visiting the zoo; St. Valentine's Day in the guise of an old-fashioned train engine, its smoke puffing hearts; a playground; football or baseball players; a dinosaur as it lived in its time and confronted with man's present-day machine world; ballerinas; TV; war; but also the family in the garden. From his trains and boats when he was twenty-six months old into his seventh year, Benjamin's interest was in machines, the machines in which people move about: on earth, in the skies, through the waters.

Benjamin had developed representationally every and any schema that he needed. Whether airplane, jet, helicopter; ships for various uses; cars and trucks; animals, from bird or sea creature to elephant and pony; man as ballplayer, child, or rock climber; tree or flower when needed, they were drawn with obvious ease. His compositional arrangements leave no doubt in the viewer. Space, often a fantastic outburst of his imagination, is based on standlines or bird's-eye-views or both combined.

Benjamin's pictures have two characteristics that make them recognizable as his individual productions from the time he was two years old through the following years: all his shapes, objects, and figures are small, all of them are distinctly outlined or contoured. In four and one-half years of picture making, he used only lines and with their help presented everything clearly, though at first not always identifiably. Another characteristic is his almost complete use of drawing space during the first seven months of his drawing activity in which he exploited every little bit of usable paper. His mother supplied him with stacks of eight- by eleven-inch scrap sheets, clean on one side, printed on the reverse.

Benjamin first shaped his objects with lines that were short, angular, and meant to represent them accurately. After a while, he interspersed his exact angular contours with curved looped lines of vivacity and life similar to his first scribble lines. Loosely and swiftly drawn, seemingly made in an uninterrupted sweep, these rounded lines showed up first in connection with waves and boats, very definitely in his little masterpiece of the "Fire Engine Boat." A year later, he used parallel curves to represent the carefully piled hay on his haytrucks.

Benjamin must have felt that lines were his way of expression, whether in monochrome with pen and pencil or in color drawings. Sometimes he combined in a single picture fine pen-and-ink technique with more robust feltpens or crayons. He began to texture parts in his pictures and, in doing so, created patterns. He gave structure to mountains or to an occasional tree; texture to the rockload carried by a truck; to race cars or to the old-fashioned little train; to the many-windowed walls of a highrise building. Lines economically characterized the giant load of raw lumber going over the freeway viaduct. His pictures, schematic but rich in content, thus became ordered in their complexity.

For examples from Benjamin's period of transition and schematic stage, view MEDIAPAK 8, frames 70-88.

(D) Benjamin's early lines and contours were not emotionally expressive. Their shortness and angularity give his drawings a sober, matter-of-fact appearance. His *involvement* with fantasies and feelings was *shown in the choice of his subjects.* His subject matter was part of his individual perception of reality, persistently shown in his drawings and the few comments he made.

From his subject preferences, we may be led to assume that he lived near the water from the time he started to draw and was quite familiar with boats and fish, and perhaps waterbirds. We also would assume that Benjamin had, on many occasions, watched trains passing by and observed them closely. In reality, however, up to age three years, eight months, he was mainly in a home environment removed from boats, trains, and waterlife. The key to the mystery of his waterlife drawings appeared to be his tiny aquarium with a few fish. His knowledge of trains and boats came from toys and pictures. From this limited experience and secondhand information, he created a fantasy world populated with what constantly occupied his thoughts. His imaginary world was not an outcome of experience in his outer environment. His picture world, a powerful reality in his mind, was closely related to wishes and dreams represented in his drawings of objects and machines.

An artist sees and feels what he creates in his inner world of imagination. So does a young child. In Benjamin's case, his earlier creations on paper all belonged to a boat-life with fish and birds, with waves, flags, and sails, in what may be called a topographical re-creation of his imagination—such as the harbor around which he could picture his other favorite interest, trains. Trains still fire the imagination of the young, point to far places where anything may happen. And it is this inner world of Benjamin's that determined the content of his pictures, their details, repeats, and elaborations. In a sense his drawing activity replaced actual play with the objects; we might say that in drawing them, he played with them. Very different from Maya, Trenton, Catharine, and other children who drew people, plants, trees, flowers, insects, Benjamin hardly ever pictured these until later.

In his pictures, Benjamin showed from early beginnings an undisturbed individualism of interest and a continuous, steady development in his style of expressing it. He added, apparently with ease, as if already clear in his mind, all that was marginal to these interests and all that related to his personal life. In doing so, he adhered to a technique that expressed his outlook and also created with it whatever was nonreal. He made it real. In his last year and one-half as a member of the study, he also was able to imbue most of his pictures with the charm that the adult admires and enjoys in folk and "primitive" art.

Module Eleven

Becky:

EMERGENCE OF FIGURES AT TWENTY-FIVE MONTHS

At the age of twenty-five months, Becky's figures emerged directly from scribbles, not from contoured shapes. (During her scribble period, before age two, she had drawn on a blackboard and scribbles, therefore, had not been recorded.) Her emerging figures can be described as scribbles that suggest shapes. They were given a skeletal understructure by some stronger, heavier lines. Becky pointed out the various parts to her mother and thus facilitated the visualization of her scribbled figure projections. Head, body, arms, and feet became recognizable as Becky named them. She drew various persons: "My Mama," "Grandma," "Baby" (her doll),

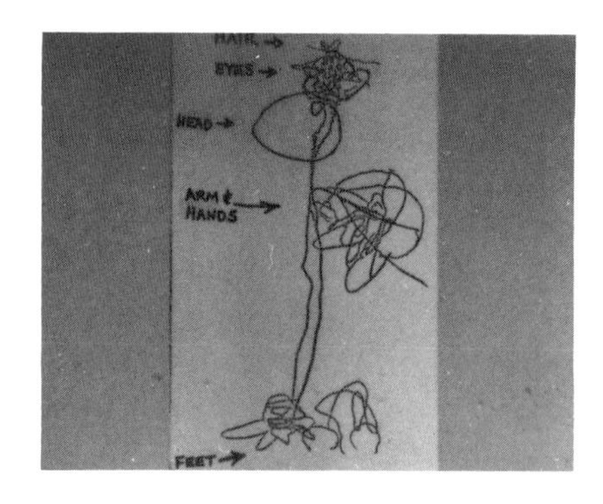

Contrary to most children, Becky's first figures emerged at twenty-five months from scribbles that might have passed as mere scribbles but for the comments she made. "Grandma" here has a head from which two legs descend. Her eyes are on top of her head. The big scribble to the right is arms and hands, the scribble at the bottom the feet.

"This is Mama," "Big Girl." An outsider may very well be hesitant to accept "Baby Doll" as a man-figure, although it looks no different from the others. But no one could doubt "Big Girl's" human form even without the detailed—and most valuable—descriptive comments by Becky. During this month of development, Becky used crayons, although later it could

An Unusually Early Development

be seen that crayons were not the most advantageous medium for the vivacity and aplomb of her lines.

From this point on, we can easily follow Becky's rapid pictorial development. She advanced in months as fast as most children do in half-years. She added details to her figures: neck, buttons and, for instance, a long "ponytail" on grandma's picture. For the most part, Becky used persons for her picture subjects, but also produced some objects that could be recognized. When, at the age of twenty-five months, she was asked by her mother to draw a pair of shoes, she produced a pair of closed shapes that clearly outlined shoe soles and looked like footprints. She drew a "Birdie" and another scribbly but unmistakeable "Duckie-birdie." Playing with a feather she had found, she drew it, not quite recognizable in shape, but suggestive of lightness and the quality of flight. She portrayed "Dog Roone," the family dog, pointing out every detail herself.

Next, Becky developed a "Ball" in a succession of drawings done in one day. She started with a circular scribble, followed by a wavering oval-shaped outline. The last ball was drawn in a single swift movement, the ends of the line crossed to close the shape. Ball shapes served Becky as catchalls that she substituted for a number of objects the shapes of which she had not yet developed.

A month later, Becky was painting such man-figures as a "Clown Sticking His Tongue Out," a "Monkey," a "Bird Flying," fish, insects, even an "Elephant." She struggled to adapt the unwieldy paints and crayons to make contour drawings. However, she also painted her feelings about "Moonlight and Stars" or the flight of airplanes in what adults would call abstracts.

Two or more Objects

At two years, two months, Becky made one of her first groups, "A Worm, a Hole for the Worm, and a Big Red Bird." At this time, Becky had discovered how to manipulate a paintbrush to achieve unambiguous lines. Her groups consisted of two or more persons or one person in conjunction with objects. She was picturing her observations and experiences. Usually, she explained to her mother the meaning of every part. Various objects in one drawing meant a statement that they belonged together. Unlike the number and variety of single, nonrelated objects that Benjamin gathered on one page, Becky's were part of one situation or event. From the start of her attempts at figures, Becky already had demonstrated that in this respect she was past the stage that Benjamin maintained for a relatively long time. Her assemblage of persons and objects had spatial inferences that we might call grouping.

For examples of Becky's early drawing development, view MEDIAPAK 9, frames 1-20.

DEVELOPMENTAL PEAK

(A) Becky's great advance in development and facility of expression occurred at the age of two years, five months. The number of drawings and paintings in this month was enormous. She now drew with feltpens that proved to be the true medium for her swift hand movements and her unwavering assurance of line. In this one month, Becky had bursts of picturing a great variety of subjects and characterizations. There is, for instance, the unmistakeable chef's hat on the "Cook" and the fat body she made him. Was this a chance happening? And her other figures: "Man With Big Feet and Too Long Hair," the paintbrush drawing of the "Man With Little Beard and Orange Hat," or "Old Grandaddy" with shaky limbs, his mouth turned down at a distinct angle. Becky's pictures seemed to supplement or even replace language. Characteristic details seemed to offer clues for what she thought. One can speculate on the events that impressed her and admire the extraordinary ways in which she attempted to give form to her thoughts and emotions.

Becky's early and incredibly fast development reached its peak when she was not quite two and one-half years old. During the next month, she began to draw more hastily and carelessly. Her development first came to a standstill, then deteriorated.

During her blitz-like development of drawing humans, Becky also envisioned objects as only older, school-age children do. She superimposed two views of a table, distinguished them by different colors—top view and side view. Among her objects, Becky drew a bicycle, scissors, toothpaste and toothbrush, and the like.

Action Pictures

Becky expressed various intentions in her picture subjects. One of them was action. Playing ball fascinated her. Some of her "Ball" pictures may have been prompted by games she saw on television, but she pictured repeatedly her friend Cathy or "A Boy" playing ball. Becky also pictured what happened in her family, such as "Mama Is Going to School" and Becky is in the picture watching her; "Everybody Is Getting Up," and others. Becky's own explanations were scribbles on the side or top of her drawing, "written" as she noted her mother writing down everything

In "Big Rock Fell on Clown's Foot," Becky shows the clown in transparency through the rock on his foot, but at right she shows the rock being thrown and uses a different finer feltpen for it.

faithfully. The number of events within the family and involving Becky seem innumerable. Other drawings recorded memorable experiences of the outside world: boys fighting, a dog chasing a cat, a girl with a swing, herself being pushed down from the slide in nursery school.

For examples of Becky's developmental peak and her action pictures, view MEDIAPAK 9, frames 21-38.

Descriptive Pictures

(B) In her action pictures, Becky's meaning of "Baby" usually is clear. In single figures or descriptive situational drawings it is not clear. At times, Becky refers to herself, at other times she refers to some small child in general, and sometimes she means her doll. Her lengthy titles enumerate and describe living things or objects and help to explain the picture. The names, mommy, daddy, grandma, clown, Cathy, and others, refer to just these persons. One day, at age two years, five months, Becky drew several pictures of small children—"Babies."

In a long parade of drawings, Becky showed her observations and commented on them: "Mommy, Her Gloves Have Buttons, Her Nose Has Nostrils," "Baby with Shoes That Have Laces," or "Baby in the Rain with Little Umbrella." Becky paid close attention to buttons or shoes and

"Old Grandaddy" must have seemed quite shaky to Becky, and she drew him here showing how weak he looked to her.

laces and other small things that interest many small children at an early drawing stage.

At this time, Becky had an important experience that she pictured in a series of drawings. She had chicken pox, and described this event in its several stages, particularly the pustules that she associated with fever and feeling hot and that she put on her drawings in heavy paint. The "dots" (for pustules) remained for a long time in her pictures although their significance was lost and they served merely as decorations.

Single Figures

After the emergence of Becky's first man-figures, single figures continued to be an important part of her output during the month of her extraordinary creativity. Her main single figure was her mother, next came grandma, daddy, grandaddy, and various small children and other characters, especially clowns of whom she drew a large number. Becky frequently drew herself with "a dimple" which she did not omit even in the unhappy position of being pushed off the slide. But she also drew people who showed an emotion, such as a "Man with Tears in His Eyes" or her "Mama with Eyes Closed."

Becky also portrayed single animals, but compared to the number of people she drew, they are few. Some of her animals are in motion, which she suggested successfully.

Like other children, Becky sometimes changed her mind while drawing. She would change a turtle partly drawn into a dog, or start with a dog but end with a "dog-faced" girl. Such turnabouts were considered by Becky as funny, jokes which she enjoyed hugely.

REPRESENTATIONAL DEVELOPMENT

How clear and recognizable did Becky's pictures grow in the four to five months of her development from the emergence of figure? They were quite primitive schemata. In fact, they could be called pre-primitive. However, most of the figures and some of the objects are recognizable, especially when helped by Becky's comments. Becky's pre-primitive phase is rather unique. Some of its characteristics belong to the state of emergence such as those of other children who then proceed directly to primitive schemata. During this pre-primitive period, perhaps because of her precocious development, Becky made a large number and a great variety of pictures. This combination allows an unusual insight into this early step of development.

During the first half of her third year, Becky evolved her man-figure and some object schemata. She interspersed these with a number of recurring but recognizable shapes that can be identified with the help of the comments she volunteered while drawing or after completing her drawing. Her development can best be traced in her man-figures. Whether man or woman or child, they were alike in appearance except perhaps for the size or some detail of clothing. Becky's man-figure had an approximately round or slightly oblong head contour with two eyes (and sometimes eyebrows), a nose, and mouth. The eyes were circles, the nose another irregular round or squarish shape or a miniature "ball" shape; the mouth was a line, sideways or straight. Ears, if present, were usually attached to the sides of the head like loops or handles. The head had some hair sticking out straight from its upper contour. It sat directly on the body which was squat with rounded edges, or oval or pear-shaped, whether placed vertically or horizontally. Arms, drawn in single lines, branched out from mid-body. Rounded patches for hands ended in a spray of fingers. Legs with feet (and toes) or shoes came down from the lower end of the body, or the feet were attached directly to the body. Becky often changed her arrangement and even forms of single parts, but the figure retained its peculiarly "Becky" character. The fact that, on developing her figure, she drew the human immediately with a body—no head-man!—is a noteworthy phenomenon. Becky also manipulated the lines of her figure drawings in a manner that the figure never appeared rigid. It seemed to bend, sit or move.

She remained fairly consistent within her own proportions unless she wanted emphasis on some part. Usually, Becky made the head one-half or one-third the size of the entire figure, on occasions twice as large. Hands and feet were large patches (hands especially) with long lines for fingers and later a thumb. She changed proportions according to the role of a particular part of the person. In the drawing of her nursery school teacher, "Miss Mary of the Nursery School," the teacher has an enormous head even when compared to Becky's usual outsized heads. The emphasis on head size frequently may be observed in drawings of older children when they draw their teacher.

Becky varied certain details of the figure to suit her interest of the moment. The nose became more and more detailed: a looped round with two tiny distinct rounds placed carefully inside—the nostrils. She often accompanied nose drawings with the admonition, "Don't pick on it." The eyes, usually empty rounds, soon were given irises, a detail Becky had observed in another child's drawing. She sometimes filled the eye rounds entirely. Becky, at age two and one-half, was eager to make profile views, explaining, "The eye and hand on the other side cannot be seen."

Becky used the ball shape she had evolved at twenty-five months as a "sign" for objects or parts of which she had not yet developed a distinctive separate schema. She adopted it, for instance, to represent a light bulb or a puddle in the rain, a record disc or a doorknob, the basket of the basketball game, or toys in a wagon—even books.

Whether she worked in pen and ink or with paints, Becky's animal schemata seemed more rigid than those of her humans. Some of them, like her "Kitticat" or "Alligator," were humanized. Others would be characterized by a detail such as the huge loop of a rabbit's ear. She drew more animals during the earliest months of her drawing activity than in her peak period. Some of her drawings appeared to be made with evident care, with clear and decisive contours. Others had unnecessarily entangled lines, perhaps caused by haste or concepts not yet clarified in a pictorial sense. Development was still visible in many drawings during the earlier part of the month following the peak at two years, five months, but Becky's activity did not result in a steady line of development or a steady pace. Deterioration started and then set in quickly.

STYLE OF REPRESENTATION

Becky's very early drawings have style—a uniquely personal, characteristic pictorial expression. Its most prominent single quality lies in Becky's dependence on lines and her consistent way of manipulating them, whether in clearly devised sweeps or in an entanglement of lines that may obscure contours and shapes. Her manner of circling, looping, interweaving lines, then fusing them into something with motion and life, gives her pictures a distinctive identity. She seemed to use her tools with such ease that by twists of the feltpen point or brush she changed from fine lines to broader ones with a single stroke. In this, as in so many ways, Becky's performance was very precocious. She reached comprehensive figure drawing at an age when most children are still absorbed in scribbles and shapes.

Many of Becky's figure drawings are so similar that at first glance they seem alike. On closer inspection, however, we can see differences in body shapes, in hands and feet, and in the drawing of heads. Similarly-drawn figures may be accentuated by a different axial direction of some single part.

The subjects of Becky's drawings may be different, but her arrangements of their various parts are surprisingly alike. She placed people and objects in a "void" since she did not indicate a groundline. However, she often placed them next to each other, their feet on an invisible base, or she put the main subject toward the center and the other figures and objects around it. Becky's drawing sheet sometimes represented the ground that extends from the bottom of the page to its top. The figures and objects close to the bottom are close to the viewer; those drawn further toward the top of the page are more distant from the viewer. Or, Becky drew a person against a void like "Cathy Playing Ball." Becky, at two years, five months, made a number of space representations that are of interest, for instance her "Restaurant."

Development was carried over as Becky reached two years, six months. Her "Mama" is a picture of uncommon liveliness and spirited expression to which the scribbly lines contributed.

The swiftness of Becky's hand movements, intimately connected with the particular style of her lines, gained momentum as time went on, so that her never-ceasing, overall mobility and liveliness of lines began to take on a hasty scribble character as she neared two years, seven months. This was at times extraordinarily effective, for example in "Mama" or "Old Grandaddy." But in contrast to this effectiveness, Becky's development was at a standstill, and soon her former expressiveness became static. She tried to find her way back by remembering her former figure representations, but in vain.

Becky's style seems to be a reflection of projecting herself into movements of people, animals, even objects. In reexperiencing these movements and reliving actions, she translated them into lines that suggest her experiences of motion and her observations of herself and others.

Relation of Figure and Ground

Up to the time of two years, six months, Becky more or less filled her drawing space. She placed single figures so that they were mainly in the center of and proportional to the paper size; or she left a comparatively large blank space, yet balanced figure and ground. Drawings with several objects often were crowded. Becky was not able to foresee how many figures and objects she would draw, or she had so many new ideas that called for expression after she started drawing that she was unable to plan her space arrangement in advance. If this happened with a single figure, she shortened the remaining part of the figure and, in some instances, she drew it "around the corner."

Importance of Picture Details

Becky had distinctive methods of showing important parts in her drawings or signaling new discoveries that she made: *size, line, color,* or a *different* medium. She usually drew hands and feet much larger in comparison to anything except the head. She rarely made them small, but if she did she called attention to this fact. Many exceptional size divergencies were difficult to understand. Perhaps Becky started on the important parts, then changed proportions because of squeeze in space.

Another way of differentiating were thick and thin lines. The use of a different medium is also perplexing at times. Sometimes the medium for a new or important part was less outstanding than the one used for other parts in contrast to the adult manner of emphasis. But to Becky, this seemed natural. Giving a different color was another way of pointing out what was important or new or signaling the difference in the character of people or objects. She made fingers, toes, buttons, toys, or purse stand out by a color different from the one she used for the rest of her picture.

Painting for Color Enjoyment

Becky made few paintings that were not drawings with paint. But she seemed to delight in color for its own sake. Her "Clown Man" is a sheer splash of brilliant red colors; so are her untitled paintings of stars, moon, and airplanes. But color also was an important way to tell, in brush drawings, about the different parts of figures and objects, point out their special meaning, or even tell some story. Her monochromes are color monochromes—the favorite colors red and green.

For examples of Becky's descriptive pictures, view MEDIAPAK 9, frames 39-72.

DETERIORATION OF DEVELOPMENT

(C) Becky made astonishing progress in drawing in five months' time. She produced beginning figures at the end of the first two months, then developed other recognizable living things and objects, added characteristic details, expanded her picture schemata, and managed to use her growing pictorial vocabulary with emphasis.

Becky's phenomenal development, however, seemed to come to a standstill after five months. First stagnation, then regression set in; she did fewer drawings and did them less well than before. Finally she reverted to scribbles.

Becky had started nursery school at twenty-nine months. The first picture she made in nursery school was a crayon drawing of faint scribble lines, a great contrast to her many home drawings that had assured strong lines. Her mother was astonished at the school drawing, so meaningless and uninteresting compared to the work done at home. Becky told her mother this was the kind of picture that "other children do." Though Becky made a series of figural drawings at home on this very same day and for the next three weeks, her school scribbles continued and seemed to be an adaptation to the lower developmental level of her older companions: scribbles and splashes.

During the next month, Becky produced a number of pen and ink drawings. Although this was the medium most suitable to her ability, she now began to use a scribble technique. In some instances it was very effective, such as in the vivid drawing of "Mama" or "Old Grandaddy" or her self-portrait with "Bump on Head." However, Becky seemed to make no advance; there was no further pictorial development. For a time, she still portrayed movement but her drawings became progressively rigid and less diversified.

Becky's present scribbly technique soon became more and more confused and confusing. She reverted to empty rounds for eyes and nose, and sometimes did not even draw the mouth. To make the body of a figure, she drew entanglements of lines that barely suggested a figure. She seemed to have lost the life-giving flexibility of her line treatment. Even her favorite subjects became weak and erratic. In fact, her mother said of one of these drawings, "Becky doesn't struggle anymore, she holds marker and brush lightly and sketches with carefree abandon." Indeed,

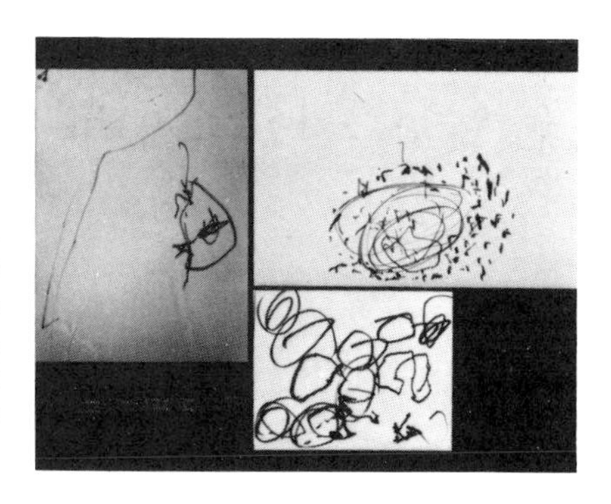

The three-inch "Squiggle" by Becky at two years, six months in a corner of a large paper otherwise left blank, marks the regression of Becky's development that continued during the next months. Like the tiny scribble with dots (center), also set in a corner of a large paper, she also made shapes (right) like these at two years, ten months.

Becky's "carefree abandon" was evident in her increased haste, lack of attention to details; it also resulted in fewer pictures that often were only half finished but that she declared to be complete. These were forerunners of the beginning deterioration in interest and care. Even her "Ball" had lost its roundness.

Now began a period of scribbles and entangled shapes per se. Placed in a corner or at the bottom of a large otherwise untouched paper, all were very small and involved, corresponding to the "squiggles," as Becky called them, that she produced in nursery school. She obviously tried hard to become one of the group in school and to avoid being "different."

Drawing development is not a steady, constant step-by-step advance. There are plateaus in development. When a new schema seems needed, there may be a lag in the level of one particular new schema compared to those already developed. In general, the phenomenon of retardation in development is more common than that of regression. For example, a fourteen-year-old may continue on the level he has reached at age nine or ten, as if he had come to a dead end. A child will seldom go back to exactly those shapes and figures he did earlier. Lori, for example, maintained three levels simultaneously for a time, scribble, shape, and emerging figure. But she did not show any signs of deterioration; in fact, she advanced in her way in each of them. Deterioration starts more often with a loss of interest in a particular medium of expression.

Becky was not on a plateau of development. At this particular time, her verbal ability possibly may have competed with her pictorial competence and overtaken it. Since she later regained drawing ability to a satisfactory degree, it may have been her desire to be one of her group, *not different,* that destroyed further progress at this point and forced her to stay on a

Becky's pictorial deterioration plainly shows in "Boy."

level entirely inappropriate for her ability. Stagnation set in, followed by deterioration and regression, the latter in the sense of Becky's attempt to perform in the scribble stage. However, her coordination, growth, maturity, and perception had not come to a standstill. Quite the contrary! Only her ability in visual communication seemed impaired. It no longer satisfied her in her nursery school environment. Verbal communication did not seem to be a source of unwanted competition. But pictorial facility did.

Becky remained in this state of deterioration for a long time, particularly surprising when compared to the extraordinary tempo of development of the preceding months. To all appearances, she persisted on staying on the level of her school companions' painting and drawing, but occasionally she returned to identifiable shapes. During the following months, she drew some former subjects in a technique similar to the past, but without its strength, almost shadows of her earlier energy and vivacity. Or she tried a new start, reminiscent of her earliest human figures.

At age three, and for a short period after, Becky's drawing activity revived a little. She started over, but these strange drawings did not reflect the sense of intensity that her former pictures imparted. She now had reached the age at which a substantial number of children start to draw figures and develop schemas, as did Kim, John, Lori, Anne, Catharine, and others of this group. The difference lies in the fact that *they started at an age after Becky had already reached a peak.* For Becky, other means of expression, other activities (such as dancing) took the place of drawing, which up to then had seemed to be her favorite and most expressive medium.

For examples of Becky's period of artistic deterioration, view MEDIAPAK 9, frames 73-85.

RENEWED START

(D) Becky, her development arrested, estranged from her former very personal and characteristic style, found herself in limbo. She did not know which avenue of expression to follow and tried several approaches in drawing and painting.

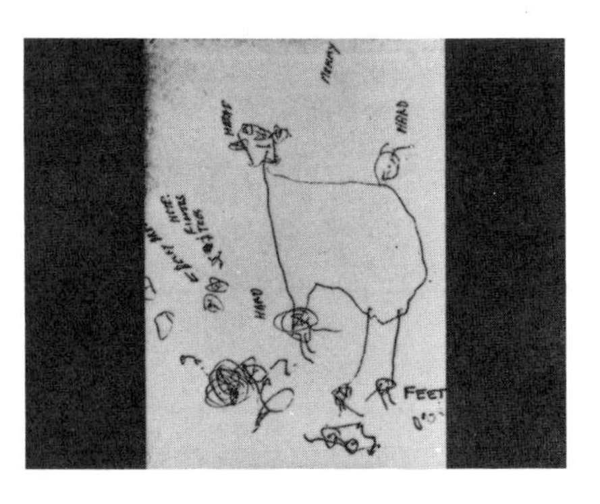

Becky's months of deteriorating picture expression seemed to regress to the scribble stage. At about age three, she tried to find a new start. One small, curious drawing, "Mommy," at two years, nine months, in pen and ink, looks like a rebirth of figure emergence.

In one way she was "tradition bound" to her past, yet she struggled toward a new start. She tried new ways of painting and drawing figures that had little in common with early Becky-figures. A "Santa Claus" series had a very different figure representation. So had "Goldilocks," a new subject interest. The difference in style can be seen in her proportions when we compare them to those of the past: now heads became small, bodies massive and ponderous. Becky's careful differentiation between arm, hand, and fingers disappeared. She now often drew them like flippers. Once in a while, Becky again drew a story or action picture.

Becky went through a long transition period during which she started in various directions. Her development was slow and irregular. So was her

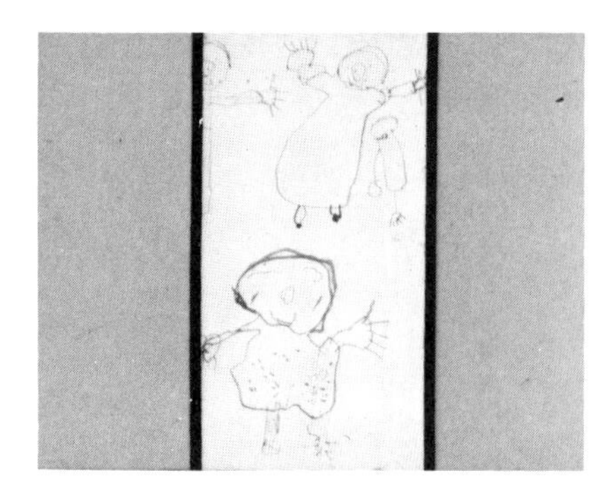

Some of Becky's figure drawings regained their vividness and were better proportioned. Here, Grandma is calling "Dinner's ready." Grandaddy is supposed to be part profile with no right arm, while Baby is entirely in profile and has only one arm and one leg. The "Clown," below, is very different from all the past clowns.

productivity. However, her principal interest was still in people. When she was nearly four, some of her figures were almost as primitive as if she just had started doing figures. Indeed, in a way it was a new emergence. But even in these attempts Becky's observation of things and her "knowledge" remained principal factors.

After age four, Becky's drawing activity revived. She became interested in trees and made long series of tree drawings. In the months after her new start, Becky again struck a high in production. Then four and one-half years old, she sometimes made many drawings in a single day. They varied in details, finish, and clarity of content. Some of them were drawn in great haste, hands and feet omitted, but most of them showed a return to a fairly easy, albeit different, swing of line that had been an early characteristic of Becky. She made girls with decorated dresses. She tried shoes with tied laces. She would set a flower next to the figures. She made nudes, robots, and monsters, a portraitlike series, but also numerous "finger families" that appeared again several months later, animals and fantasy drawings like dreams, even still lifes and flower people.

Copying or drawing a model directly after it is shown is still the subject of research for various reasons, one of them being to judge the differences in perceptive observation and reproduction of what has been perceived. A simplified, that is, geometrical, figure may be used as model, for instance the figure of a diamond. Essentially, the manner in which the model is "copied" or drawn from memory is related to whether or not or how far the child has comprehended it and how he represents it, also showing how closely the total figure has been retained. To a small child a geometrical figure is comparatively meaningless. He tries to enliven it by imagining it as something real—a square is a house, a circle a ball or a face. If left to themselves, children will add some realistic details: windows to the square, eyes and mouth to the circle, etc. They "complete" the abstract form and give it a meaningful content. Becky proceeded in this manner. Her mother wanted to find out how well Becky reproduced the geometrical shape of a diamond that she showed to her. Becky, then in her fifth year, was able to draw it quite correctly. Repeating it, she used it as outline for a face, even added hands to it. Some months later, Becky returned on her own to the diamond contour and made of it a face with geometrical features, arms, legs, etc.

The irregularities of Becky's picture achievements, her return to a less developed state especially in drawing people, her renewed development from then on, were observed until she was over six and one-half years old. At an unusually early age, Becky had shown understanding for spatial relations, although the ways she pictured them were difficult to decipher. Now she started to render space relations in the manner young children usually do—a clear earth-to-sky arrangement. She aligned figures and objects in elevation on an earth- or groundline, left an empty space for air, and drew the sun and a strip of sky on the top of her page. She also combined alignment with bird's-eye views.

Her large amount of Christmas drawings at age five, which took three months to progress from a crude tree drawing to more and more refined and detailed pictures of this subject, was obviously an activity she greatly enjoyed. During her seventh year, some of Becky's tree drawings gained in richness. A tree now showed branches full of leaves and blossoms with grass, flowers, and a figure below and the sun shining above. Becky elaborated on her people, such as her "King and Queen," or made a full and complex interior, or a picture of her family and of her friends, entire scenes with houses, trees and sun, what she saw in the zoo, and drew many other experiences and observations. Her technique has visibly improved. She drew in fine lines and in a way similar to Benjamin who lived half a continent away.

Although Becky's interest in picture making had decreased disappointingly after age two and one-half, other interests replaced it. The strongest factor in self-expression was her verbal ability. When her pictorial ability revived, Becky did not follow a steady direction. She seemed to explore all kinds of by-paths, various possibilities that she again abandoned, returned to, and tried to connect with past "methods" and then also abandoned. However, once she had turned away from her regressive scribbles and interested herself once more in people, she again developed figure drawing and represented living things and objects, but differently from the past.

By the time Becky reached age four and during the next two years, her pictorial development compared favorably with that of other children of her age, and her production again was sizable. It seems that her interest in subject matter, in demonstrating her knowledge of things surrounding her, quite in keeping with her critical attitude, tended more toward verbal expression. Furthermore, her lack of interest in careful execution or accomplished technique that improved only during the last year and one-half of participation in the study, points to a minor role in purely visual expression for her future.

For examples of Becky's renewed start in art, view MEDIAPAK 10, frames 1-35.

(E) Becky's early pictures are an unusual presentation of the inner life of a very young child, particularly between two and two and one-half years. They are direct, spontaneous, and extraordinarily numerous communications about herself. In them she discloses her observational powers and her vivid participation and response to all kinds of circumstances. Although plant and insect life and their wonders did not seem to affect her as they did other children discussed in this program, her delight in nature expresses itself in many pictures of the wonders of the heavens. For one so small, Becky's expression of these feelings in pictures is unique. And it offers a unique opportunity for adults to gain insight not only into the delights, emotions, discoveries, but also the observational and reasoning powers of one so young and her ability to share them by direct communication.

Module Twelve

The Brothers:

Claude and Paul, brothers two and one-half years apart in age, are among the very young whose development of pictorial expression is very different from Becky's or Benjamin's or that of the other children described in this longitudinal research. Their art work is remarkable because many of their early achievements merit the adult description of *aesthetic*.

Aesthetic accomplishments of the kind seen in Claude's pictures and also those of Paul may be described as a particular sense of form and shape and of technique in relation to medium. Within the framework of childhood art, Claude and Paul achieved artistic effects which appear to have been intended goals. This is in contrast to the aims other children deem important, such as telling a story or describing things in nature or expressing emotions or spinning out fantasies. Claude's and Paul's aesthetic results were achieved mainly by simplification of form for the purpose of "beauty" and partly by decoration and embellishment. Their work retained the character of child art, but they used ingenious techniques of grouping or positioning and color combinations within that character.

In the past, child art was looked upon mostly, if not entirely, as a steplike development of representational skill leading eventually to the adult view of a realistic representation of people and things. The widely-held concept that children's art efforts are the beginning steps toward adult art, that this is the purpose of their art, had led to being thus valued and judged. Child art has not been considered as something separate, consistent and satisfying in its own right. In recent years, a new appraisal and appreciation of child art on its own terms has gained wider acceptance. The studies of Lowenfeld and many others after him shifted evaluation by regarding the emotional content as a central force in child art. A long time before, Cizek had described child art as an art in itself, a phase of childhood to be looked upon separately from the art of adults. Piaget, in a general manner that includes art, does much the same.

Claude

STYLE OF PICTURING

Comparatively indifferent to pictorial story content or descriptive visualization of people or objects, Claude, in his earliest years, showed little interest in drawing facts, "real" nature. Many children, at the time they enter school and earlier, treat subject matter based on reality, yet elaborate them by decorative means. Numerous examples of it can be seen in the pictures of the children here, all made between ages three and six. Although decorative, with embellishments, they are meant to be realistic.

Claude's designs are abstractions and have an unreal quality. Even the few early shapes his mother kept showed what one might call a *disciplined* use of line and paint for a definite goal in terms of form. Claude submerged the realistic appearance of plants, animals, objects, or man by creating a

Claude's early preoccupation with form is seen here. The looped, wide brush strokes, twice underlined by horizontals, are like an introduction to his decorative style. Without the thin, downward runs of color, we would not know that a two-year-old painted them who had not yet found the right consistency for his paints.

formal aspect which strengthened the feeling for the interaction of ground and figure. This formal quality may seem to be illusive, unrealistic or abstracted, yet it represents the relevant characteristic of Claude's experiences. As a consequence, or because of it, there is a diminished tendency to represent things in terms of realism.

Claude clearly aimed toward an aesthetically satisfying result. He tried a great variety of design subjects. Their source may be seen in his intensive observation of details on living things, especially plants and insects. In this sense, many of his designs are based on reality. He deliberately abstracted from his original source an essence that gave his art an unreal core. Usually, he made entire series of designs based on a central concept of line and color that he developed and perfected. One could observe this manner of work as early as age three. With a color scale in mind, he tried sequences of circles and ovals encased in one another and parallel winding

Three-year-old Claude drew human figures, although rarely. From the start, he either treated them decoratively as here in "Vittorio" or used them as he used any other motif for ornamental designs.

lines that he pursued until satisfied with the result. He worked out sequences of this nature for various "flower-" or "insectlike" designs; for instance, the intriguing architectonics of spider webs or shells. His simple head-man, like insect or flower, was used in experiments for designs. But Claude also experimented with painted dots, horizontal lines, and combinations of both using large sheets, sophisticated color combinations, and appropriate backgrounds for them. Through ages four and five, he also made large numbers of related linear designs, brush painted, trying various

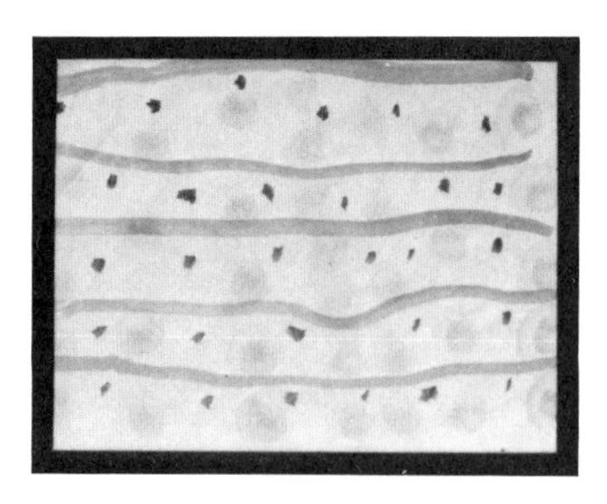

Claude, at age five, made many dot and line paintings. This one is on pink ground. Here the dots are like flat small disks.

techniques with an intuition for color, shades, and shapes amazing for one so young.

The number of Claude's abstracts decreased as he got older. At age six and from thereon he made fewer entirely abstract pieces. Because of his intense interest in anything of nature, his keen observation led him to follow day-by-day growth of plant-, insect-, and birdlife. He expressed these observations by creating lines and forms that derived from real appearances in structure and coloring, but which he "formalized." Essentially, he simplified and shaped the nature of whatever living thing he studied to conform to his own way of thinking and feeling.

As Claude grew older, he became deeply involved in fantasies related to his inner experiences of life, religion, and the feelings he shared with all living creatures. Later, at about age nine, he became interested in the mechanical world of man and made fictional pictures of cars and trucks, exteriorized fantasies related to them, and sometimes added something of the plant or animal world. These, too, were formalized to some extent and carried out with the skill of a craftsman.

Claude was not articulate about his pictures and seldom gave verbal explanations or direct titles. He said that he *liked* to do pictures this way. However, he was willing to explain technical procedures or the nature of the medium as he saw it, and did so lucidly. In his ninth year and later, Claude's pronounced degree of self-training became obvious with his change in subject matter. His eye, schooled by observation, and his skill, refined by self-discipline and patience, served him for whatever his undertaking was, for instance his nature studies or science fiction subjects.

For examples of Claude's designs, view MEDIA-PAK 10, frames 36-66.

MEDIA AND TECHNIQUE

(A) In Claude's case, we cannot separate his grasp of medium from his technique in using it, nor can the matter of figure-ground relation be separated from his very personal and individual style of arriving at his design. They were intertwined, interdependent and inseparable. The result was a unified, unique style of his own.

In drawing and painting, Claude used many different tools and materials. The central reason for his successful accomplishments, apart from an intuitive feeling for the medium, may well have been an implied understanding of the important role of technique for the realization of an idea. Furthermore, Claude must have been aware of the destructive effect of haste and neglect. Indeed, we might be tempted to discuss his technique and achievements without regard to the age factor.

Claude's drawing techniques were mainly based on the use of fine-pointed tools: pen, color pencils, and fine-point feltpens. His linear designs were in one, two, or more colors, mostly on papers and cardboards of only five by eight inches or smaller. He made series of linear abstracts with fantastic blossoms and leaves, series of insect-derived designs, and geometrical experiments with spherical elements such as shells. He painted tiny rounds in rows or winding lines with assured strokes, completed to perfection, but always with enough irregularity to give it life. Matched, long parallel snakelike lines proceeded unerringly. He carefully calculated the color effects of the pencils and feltpens against ground color or ground texture. He also used color outlines or dots for varying background textures.

Claude expressed aesthetic concepts differently when he painted on large papers. Technically, he adapted his brush strokes in width and manipulation to the size of his paper. He seemed to adjust the width of his stroke to his compositional concept when using line technique. His patterns required great eveness of execution, time, and perseverance. For a child between two and five, his many painted and dotted patterns show a great degree of ability in handling brush and paint.

In addition to the paint and brush medium and fine-pointed tools used for linear treatment, Claude used other media with success. One of these was egg tempera, another was blow technique with paints. In this latter, a small amount of ink or watercolor is poured on the paper, then, with a straw, the liquid is blown on the sheet in various directions. Many children of Claude's and Paul's age delight in this playful technique and the entirely accidental splashy designs resulting from it. Although the liquid can be channelled at will to form shapes or slender lines, most children are unable to use any control. Claude, and later Paul, not only attained

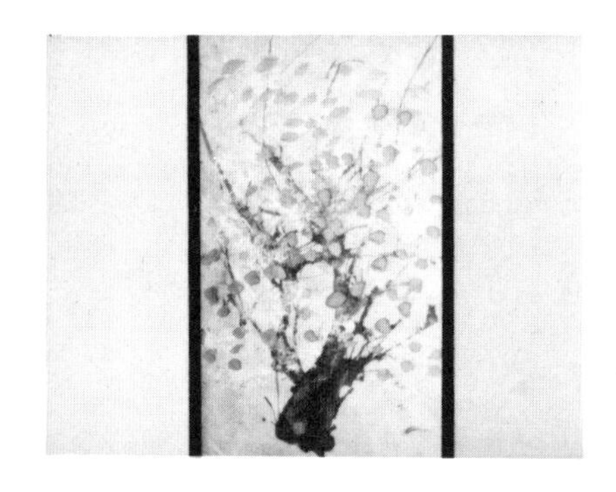

Claude's "Tree in Bloom" stands against a background of subdued colors. Claude followed logically the tree's growth with his blow technique, first the trunk and branches, next the green leaves, and finally he dabbed on the blossoms.

great control of the blowing process, but were able to produce intended fantastic forms of trees and bushes. They painted backgrounds first in vivid bands of color or delicate shades, then made the shapes they had planned. Effects of this kind not only need forethought but also control of the medium. The *artistic* results achieved by the two brothers using this technique were amazing. Claude used additional techniques, for instance in producing a blossoming tree. The first impression of this particular piece on the adult is that of a Japanese print, but Claude had never seen Japanese art. On closer inspection, we become aware of the simplicity and immediacy of child's work.

Another technique with which Claude experimented successfully was a dipped-string technique, which kindergarten children also enjoy because of its accidental surprise effects. After one-half of a folded paper is covered with the string design, the two sides are closed together when still wet. Thus, a matching imprint is made on the formerly blank half-side and the result is a symmetrical mirror-reversed effect. Claude, by very careful and skillful manipulation, produced some exquisitely delicate effects, some of them in the shape of bird shadows. The complexity of his patterns far outranks the much publicized "computer" patterns of a few years ago that, next to Claude's work, look crude and unoriginal.

Claude tried a number of other media and techniques, such as dribble painting or combining crayon and pasted-on, twisted, three-dimensional paper shapes. He continued only with those media that satisfied his aims and quality of execution. This also generally was true of other children in this study; experimenting with different media was fun, but each child continued with such a particular medium only when it served his own intentions and self-development.

Color was an important factor in Claude's aesthetic approach. It seemed to be an ever-present thought in his creative work, whether in outline or structural details. It seemed to dominate his monochromes and showed in his discrimination of choice of color grounds. Sometimes the design seemed to be a monochrome at first sight, but one discovered that Claude subtly had added tiny bits of secondary colors.

PICTORIAL ARRANGEMENT

Claude's style can be further described by the manner in which he disposed of the space on which he drew or painted. Unlike most children of his age, he did not consider the ground to be a meaningless void, unimportant, while the figure was all that counted. He recognized the interrelationship of figure and ground in making a picture. He also seemed to place his figure with great care in the available space, sometimes by providing a large space around it and indicating limits with a frame, as in his "Quail." The need to center or off-center the main part of the picture is also seen. Like most very young children, he tended toward symmetry. However, he often accentuated the right and left side of the picture and treated the central part, if at all, as a link between them. He applied the same care he exercised in his abstractions to any composition, page arrangement, or use of tools and media. He showed preference for small, often quite tiny sizes.

In addition to trying for aesthetically satisfying solutions, whether abstract or semiabstract, Claude made a number of pictures directly derived from nature and reality. In most of them, he simplified certain aspects and stressed decorative characteristics. In contrast to his "Designs," these pictures show a distinct relationship to what attracted him in nature. Here also, his goal was toward an aesthetic solution that satisfied him.

In his series of "Volcanoes," Claude made one with an entirely simplified mountain shape and indicated the activity of the volcano with a few lines in red and blue issuing from the top.

Like most other children, he led a life of fantasy along with his "real" life. This coexistence is documented visually in his art and vividly in his concepts of animal- and plantlife. One of the most engaging painted expressions of this kind is his "A Proposito del Paradiso"—"The Graceful Birds." The idea of plants being like people occurred to him frequently, as seen in his tree with a face that extends a branch-hand to a chrysanthemumlike flower's convoluted root-end above ground. The message appeared to be brotherhood. A long series of "Trees Growing Suns" illustrates other fantasies.

Claude liked to combine plants and animals in his pictures. When he placed flowers and birds or insects together, the flowers seemed to have bird- or insectlike qualities, or insects and birds a flowerlike character.

A collection drawn with feltpens is "Fruit of the Moon." It has simplified forms, each different, and reflects Claude's fantasies on this subject carried out carefully and lovingly.

When eight years old, he made a collection of drawings he called "Flora and Fauna." Derived from nature, they were unrealistic, things of his imagination. So was his still more fantastic series, "Fruit of the Moon."

For examples of Claude's formalization of pictures, fantasy pictures, media, and techniques, view MEDIAPAK 10, frames 67-96.

REPRESENTATIONAL DEVELOPMENT

(B) For Claude, reality seemed evasive though present. Abstraction was often only partial, but noticeable. Man-figures became formalized and remained "primitive." Humans were looked upon as design elements, not different from blossoms or leaves.

Claude's scribbles had not been retained. The few that existed at age seven belong to a stage in which they served to consciously express an emotion. Few of his shapes were available, already having definitive design qualities. Future aesthetic goals appear in many series on specific subjects and show his tendencies toward abstract expression. For a child of two and three, the assurance with which these pieces were executed is impressive.

Claude started at age three to make trees with leaves, fruit, and blossoms, flowers and animals, people and houses. He continued to do so at four and five. The development—or discovery?—of the human figure may have been derived from the sun, since all the first heads have rays around the

Claude painted this group of his mother, himself in front of her, and baby Paul on her arm against a textured background when he was four.

"face," but the rays can also be interpreted as hair or legs. His flower people are man-figures, head-men with blossoms for heads and stems for legs. He made a few real man-figures. When he wanted to, he could make a crowd of people as he did at age five in his "Escara Fountain of Rome."

At five and during his sixth and seventh years, Claude made animals, trees, flowers, houses with doors and chimneys, series of volcanoes, and airplanes. These pictures are "representational," partly simplified, sometimes abstracted, but all derived from his study of nature. Man remained a byproduct, part of Claude's rather large concept of nature and its creations. Claude's emotional participation seemed indirect, sometimes showed in titles, sometimes was described in his mother's comments.

Claude's interpretation of space may be seen as early as age four when occasionally he made standlines, one above the other. However, it is questionable whether the standlines indicate "near" and "far" or whether they, too, are a pattern. He used grass for ground- or standlines and marked the line of horizon between water and sky by color differentiation. His vivid "Apple Harvest" has proportioned space, everything in it—cart, boxes, driver, ladder, appletree—seen from one viewpoint. Not so in his colorful painting "First Classroom" in which front, back, side, and top views are mixed, yet presented so that one can understand its meaning.

Claude's proportions were the disproportions of the schema: a flower reached as high as the roof or was as large as a tree or twice the size of a child. Houses were transparent. He also, however, made perfectly proportioned, nonschematic living things and objects. We can observe this variety of representation by Claude at age four as well as at age ten.

Like many other children, Claude displayed a definite sense of humor, although even his humorous pictures were subject to ornamental modifications and had design qualities.

For examples of Claude's representational development, view MEDIAPAK 11, frames 1-23.

(C) Claude continued his art activities at home through his first school years uninfluenced by his school experiences in art. With his early, self-developed techniques and mastery of media, he could express his new interests as they arose, for instance cars and airplanes and science fiction drawings. He also continued his drawing studies of nature with an adult approach. Although art activity was not anymore a dominating interest or principal way of expression, Claude worked with the same intricacy of technical skill, taste in color, and knowhow that he had shown and developed from age two on.

Claude presents an unusual, we even might say extraordinary, case of child art. Representationally, he was not different from nor did he excel other children of his age. But in artistry, self-instigated and self-developed, he was exceptional. Art for him was not a picture language suitable for various ends. Like words are of importance for a poet because all depends on *how* he says what he finds necessary to say, so for Claude the *form* of his picturing seemed more important than the subject matter.

Module Thirteen

The Brothers:

Claude's younger brother Paul also seemed to have an aesthetic aim. The similarity cannot be defined. It appears to show in Paul's simplified and patternized forms of plants and objects. Paul, two and one-half years younger than Claude, developed his picture expression mainly from age five on.

STYLE

Paul's style of picturing is predominantly decorative, yet the charm of his art seldom if ever is found in abstract designs. He kept to factual contents, living or man-made, but had definite concepts of the form in which to represent them. The "aesthetic" appearance of many of his drawings and paintings is due to the kind of schemas he created, their compositional arrangement, technique, and size. We might come closer in describing its nature by calling it stylized.

Paul's subject matter was more limited and repetitive than Claude's. His pictorial conception of the subject is striking and so is his firm adherence to it. He created a few schematic shapes of living things and objects and carried them out in a technique and in arrangements of his own. His many sequences of the same content in schematic representation and composition appear to be more a play with variations on a theme than attempts to gain a better final solution.

Composition in Paul's pictures seems to start at approximately age five with simple groupings that are more or less symmetrical. There is his favorite theme, repeated over and over in drawings and paintings: "Boy-in-His-House." Its content is just what the title says, a house, an armless boy inside it, a small tree, and a high flower on each side of the house.

Paul

Trees were Paul's other favorite subject. He usually placed a single tree judiciously within the available space, branches spread evenly, symmetrically, horizontally. On these branches, like birds aligned on telephone wires, he drew identical leaves in regular order. "Designs" are designs only because of the multiple, repetitive arrangement of a single motif or a small group of things. Paul pictured these in various sizes but in the same shape and character. He made long series of trees, all similar, all done in

"Boy-in-His-House" pictures all boys or witches as armless and alike except for the witch's dunce cap. Houses have one or two windows, are transparent, have a tree on one side, and a tree-size flower on the other side.

the same technique, all set on paper in the same manner. His long series of houses or cars resemble one another in technique, size, and settings. In some of these pictures he made actual things, patternlike, accentuated by the same medium and a technique of drawing of parallel contours, of parallel structural lines, arranged in a chain or in rows on one or several planes. Abstract drawings have a motif taken from nature. Paul filled the space with an "unreal" form of the motif, or with endless repetitions of it. His drawings on any given subject of his choice were serializations, like monologues told in images.

MEDIUM AND TECHNIQUE

Paul used the same media as his older brother, but not in the same order of preference. Like Claude, he favored small sizes, some even tiny, as small as two or three inches. He drew in careful, fine lines with pen or pencil, in a single color or in many, but he seemed committed almost rigidly to the technique he chose. When he painted, he used large sizes. He managed his brush as if it were a big, heavy, delineating tool. He applied strong, often unusual colors, using the same characteristic brush strokes. His vivid color combinations often were unexpected. Sometimes, by using thin paint, he suggested lightness. He still remained indifferent to the actual color of things at an age when his brother and other children took notice and recorded them. However, unlike other children, his color choices were not dictated only by favorite colors. He showed a keen awareness of their mutual effectiveness. His paintings appear to be conceived and composed in a similar manner as his small-sized linework, but adjusted to medium and size. This parallelism in concept can be observed particularly clearly in his subject of "Boy-in-His-House" and its variations which remained a favorite for about a year and one-half.

Differences between Paul and Claude showed in the very strong, vivid colors of Paul's earliest shape paintings. Claude also had vivid colors in some representational paintings such as his "Apple-Harvest" or his purple tree, yet the character of vividness is different from Paul's. Paul's blow technique pieces are rather similar in structure to Claude's, but some of his watercolor backgrounds are distinctly set apart.

Paul worked mostly with the same materials as his brother. However, he achieved decorative qualities very different from those of his brother and those of other children in this study. One must keep in mind that whatever technique and medium Paul used, Claude had used them two or more years earlier; when Paul became engrossed in their use, Claude was no longer involved in them.

PICTORIAL ARRANGEMENT

Paul's pictorial arrangements were based on repetition of a motif, its details and embellishments. The motif was slightly varied but, like his innumerable "Boy-in-His-House" drawings, show similarity at one glance. This is equally true of his paintings on this and other subjects such as trees. The colors differ, the structure and composition remain. Similarly, in his witch subject that occupied him greatly and was directly connected with "Boy-in-His-House," the witch either replaces—pictorially speaking—the boy or is a parallel interwoven with it. She looks like the boy schema, her only distinguishing attribute a peaked hat. The emotional situation is characterized by the witch never directly associating with the boy, but being separated in place; for example, with the boy in the house, the witch is in the attic. This, however, does not alter the compositional arrangement of this subject. As for other subjects, Paul planned these paintings with regard to his choice of ground, occasionally painting the ground in a pattern or giving it texture.

Paul's "Trees" all have the same structure and directionality of branches. Directionality, as used here, refers to children's earliest attempts at stating principal directions in simplest terms: vertical and horizontal direction for living things. The vertical may be symbolic of the upward reach, the

During his sixth year, Paul made trees, trees, trees, some with and some without roots. He also drew many flowers.

growth from the ground toward the sky. The horizontal may signify expansion, spread parallel to the earth. Thus, in early man drawings, legs attached to the head (or body) are given a vertical direction; arms, whether placed at the ears, mid-body, or shoulders, emerge horizontally. Trees show this simplification of direction especially clearly: the trunk is vertical, the branches horizontal. Details, such as twigs, grow from the branches at 90 degrees, thus extend again in a vertical direction. Later, the child modifies the horizontals and secondary verticals (twigs) by giving them a slant. Still later, he bends or twists branches into individual growth patterns. Catharine's early Christmas cards and Kim's early trees clearly demonstrate this primary directionality.

Some of Paul's trees were infinitely small. Medium and technique were carefully adjusted to size. Their decorative, unreal effect is all-pervasive both in medium and technique. So are his nearly identical flowers, whether drawn or painted.

When Paul became interested in cars, he made series of them. Here, again, as with his houses, we can observe that they all are identical in

The subject of these "Racing Cars" in red pen could be a showroom or a race. The small cars in the row on top have no drivers. In most car series, the wheels and drivers' hair are patterned. Some drivers have hands.

shape and in manner of drawing; they are formalized. They differ visibly from object schemata of this kind by other children. The formalization of his car drawings in conjunction with their row arrangement on one or more planes, the treatment of the lines with which they were drawn, are central to the unrealistic quality of form imparted by Paul's work. He applied a similar treatment to the roofs of his houses. The results in both—and in others—have the same effect that can be seen later in his fish, birds, or mountain drawings.

For examples of Paul's series of the boy in his house and trees, view MEDIAPAK 11, frames 24-48.

(A) Paul's imagination and fantasies tended toward animals and their social life. Oddly, he often connected them with a very human habitat, the house. Among his drawings are a "Fantasy House," a "Fish School" and a "Worm-House," the latter in the shape of an apple. "Easter Day in the Park" is celebrated by a bird population carried on a wagon. Some

The tiny drawing of this "Fish School" by Paul shows a large house filled with fish, one of them very big (the teacher?). Birds are perched on the roof hoping for a chance to catch and eat them.

of his trees and many of his flowers are humanized. Whimsically, like "Boy-in-His-House," he even drew some pictures of "Tree in the House." Other fantasies show a scarecrowlike "Monster" crowned by a gigantic machinelike head; if it had been drawn by an adult, it would be seen as a caricature of our present, machine-obsessed time.

At age seven, perhaps because of his brother's "fictional cars," Paul made some startling, fantastic cars, though quite different from those done by his brother. He injected humor.

For examples of Paul's fantasy pictures, view MEDIAPAK 11, frames 49-65.

REPRESENTATIONAL DEVELOPMENT

(B) Paul's fantasy pictures were based on a representational approach. His representational development was similar to that of Claude and that

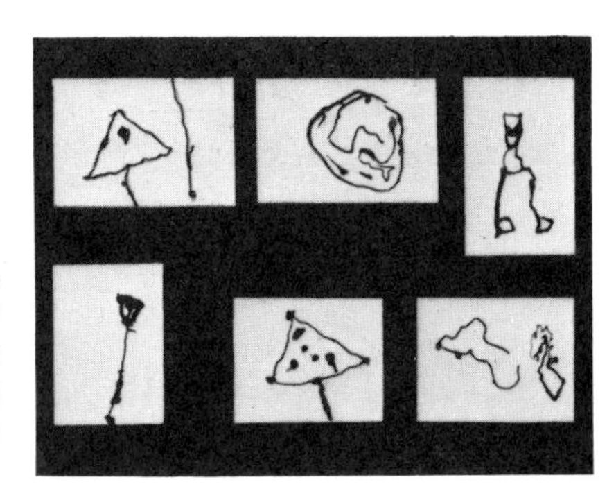

Between ages four and five, Paul drew many tiny shapes, most of which point to development of figures, plants, or animals. The pen drawing at upper right is meant to be a figure; the one at the lower left a tuliplike flower, and next to it a tree; at the lower right corner is an animal.

of other children. At the start, he worked out man-figure, plant, and animal by experimenting with tiny abstract lines and shapes. Among these, as Paul reached ages three and four, we can perceive the beginning shapes of humans, trees, and objects. His man-figures, repeated almost identically for boy, man, or witch, were given some single distinguishing attribute like the duncecap of the witch. Each figure consisted of a roundish contour for the head, usually bald, dots for eyes, a large upward curve for the mouth, and perhaps a button nose. The head sat directly on the body, which was U-shaped or squarish and sometimes filled out solidly. Two single-lined legs were attached to the body and had loops for feet. Surprisingly, at age five and part of age six, Paul drew no arms for his boy figures or witches, especially when he placed them inside his house or, particularly noticeable, as drivers of cars. He developed animals and composite flowers, often with human faces. Sometimes he painted them; at other times, he drew them in line technique.

The house was Paul's main concern, a constantly repeated subject. Its schema did not vary: one see-through wall, a window and door, or both, or no wall at all, and a roof that fitted tightly with no eaves. This very characteristic roof form with no overhang has been observed through decades in young children's untaught drawings of houses. When Paul added a chimney, he placed it at a right angle to the roof slant, another characteristic shared with other children of the present and the past.

All through Paul's drawings, trees appeared more often than any other single thing. For years they remained essentially the same. He outlined a very sturdy trunk, set flat on the ground of a short horizontal line

Paul continued to make more of the tiny drawings like the ones shown here. Plants, blossoms, and the "Bird in His House" have definite characteristics that we can identify.

like the base of an object. He occasionally made the roots. He drew the branches horizontally, carefully distanced from one another,and adorned them with identical leaves in a row. The horizontal direction of the branches changed gradually toward an upward slant and finally to near vertical at the crown, thus forming a rounded silhouette. No twigs grew from the branches. The schema on this subject remained in its fundamental form, the simplest shape, yet every tree is a very decorative piece of artwork.

Tree, house, and human are described in detail because, in Paul's art, they seemed to occur constantly and to be closely related to his life. His ever-repeated "Boy-in-His-House" groups represent this favorite scene in representational arrangements based on an earth-to-sky concept. One small drawing, made when he just turned eight, shows in clear lines how far he had developed: a well-proportioned human figure, a house, now showing three sides, a tree with a birdnest on top, and a huge flower all set on a grassy undulating groundline and blessed by an enormous sun with which Paul here identified himself.

Similar to other children in their early schematic stage, Paul pictured proportions that were entirely nonrealistic: a flower the size of a house was quite usual. However, in his art this arbitrary, unreal manner of proportion became integrated in the design as if planned to serve a decorative, aesthetic consideration. When Paul's approach was representational, as it was often in his human shapes, his proportions were less incorrect—he seldom placed a huge head on a tiny body.

Among Paul's representational drawings are a number of vessels and baskets. Paul drew them with great skill and emphasized their shape and pattern. He made a series of vases with flowers in them. Drawn with color pencils, he showed an unusual understanding for their shapes and an equally unusual taste in the placement of the flowers they contained. These very small-sized studies were made with patience and finesse.

Paul, like Claude, continued to develop his particular art forms at home, away from the school curriculum that they both thoroughly disliked. The brothers continued in their own way up to ages eight and ten. In doing so, they maintained their individual character, satisfied their own needs of expression, and pursued the quest for understanding the world around and within themselves.

For examples of Paul's representational development, view MEDIAPAK 11, frames 66-83.

TESTS OF INTELLECTUAL ABILITIES OF FOUR CHILDREN

(C) From their biographies, Benjamin, Becky, Claude, and Paul emerged as highly individual youngsters who share not only involvement in art expression but other characteristics as well. The four were given intelligence tests and emerged again with certain shared similarities. All four tested in the superior range: two on the Wechsler and two on the Stanford Binet. All four showed superior vocabulary and language reasoning.

Interestingly enough, in some early research on children's art, before the general use of intelligence tests, it was observed that most children "gifted in art" were bright, but bright children were not necessarily good in art. No doubt most of our thirty children seem to exceed "normal" intelligence, but only four were followed through with actual testing at the time of the study.

At the time of testing, Paul, Claude, Becky, and Benjamin scored not only well above average, but also above their own performances in structural nonverbal tests. In view of the creative productivity of these children, it is interesting to note how closely language skills parallel art ability. This suggests a challenge to teachers and parents to regard young children's art efforts more for their implicit communication and their revelation of children's interests and concerns than for their aesthetic value. This further suggests that fluency of line and cursive patterns are natural movements in children's early art activity. Certain educational systems have favored the cursive approach to writing since it builds on the natural skill and to some extent can help some children with weak hand-eye coordination to get around the difficulties inherent in copying and learning the script writing. Good visual motor coordination and legible writing are generally important in academic success.

At the time of the testing, two children showed some immaturity in eye-motor coordination in tasks requiring immediate recall and copying; yet Benjamin was able to draw, at age two, long complex lines with unwavering assurance. Tested at age three years, seven months, Benjamin seemed comfortable in the test situation and showed promising vocabulary and verbal reasoning. His creative ability was demonstrated in the next several years, and by his seventh year his schoolwork verified the test's forecast for later high academic achievement.

Paul, when tested at seven years, one month, also showed some immature visual-motor coordination, but verbal ability and reasoning were well advanced. Though he had drawn few figures, he worked hard on the Goodenough *Draw-a-Man* test, as though he had some self-criticism and wanted to do his best. Despite his art activities, he was somewhat weak in visual alertness, visual memory, and the coding tasks that involve hand-eye coordination. Both these auxiliary skills are involved in learning to read and may have affected somewhat his otherwise quick and comfortable reading comprehension.

Becky, who was tested at three years, five months, also offers an interesting parallel to the other children. She passed all language and visual-motor items up to the four and one-half-year level. At the five-year level, she was unable to make an exact square, making rounded corners instead of right angles. However, she was able to analyze a simple maze and could plan a route showing that she was aware of the difference between a short and a long way through it. She also had difficulties with the angles and sharp corners of another aspect of the test. But in her home drawings, a few months later, she successfully made diamonds and even animated this one-time difficult shape with facial features, arms, and legs, revealing the imaginative and humor-loving side of her thought processes. She could describe what was happening in a picture and was ready to play word games of any kind. Her thinking, direct and economical, suggested later academic success. This forecast of academic skills was confirmed as predicted because of the very early verbal facility and general ability to conceptualize that showed in the test.

Claude emerged from the test, which he took at nine years, eight months, showing superior intellectual abilities, highly motivated, and interested and involved in constructive and creative thinking (so well shown in the science fiction pictures made at home at this time). He was especially good at planning and following a visual pattern (very apparent in his early decorative art activity), and executing a task that required visual-motor organization. For the *Draw-a-Man* test, he made "a happy hippie," perhaps reflecting that he himself was underchallenged in school and somewhat on the outside of his peer group. On the test, he did well in practical logic and social insight items. He was critical of his school's structural art program where he felt underchallenged. In his home environment, which offered freedom for creative opportunities, he set high goals for himself that he followed through successfully.

The parallels which these four children offer are interesting and provocative, but their number is far too small to permit any general conclusions to be drawn.

Part Five

The Impact of Preschool: What Can Be Done to Encourage Child Art?

Module Fourteen

The Lesson of

"He Pushed Becky Off the Slide" is one of fourteen drawings and paintings made on a single day at home after her first drawing in nursery school. Becky's first school drawing, called "Snowstorm," has *weak* crayon *lines* and is shapeless, a scribble. In contrast, her fourteen homemade drawings have different subjects: a "Baby with Toys All Around," a "Funny Looking Girl," a "Little Black Baby with Red Buttons," another drawing of herself having been pushed off the slide, a "Little Baby Has a Little Bitty Bicycle," a "Cook," and others. They are figural schemas, primitive, but done in *decisive* lively *lines.*

Obviously, Becky had much on her mind, felt strongly about her experiences, and tried to show them in her drawings and comments. The draw-

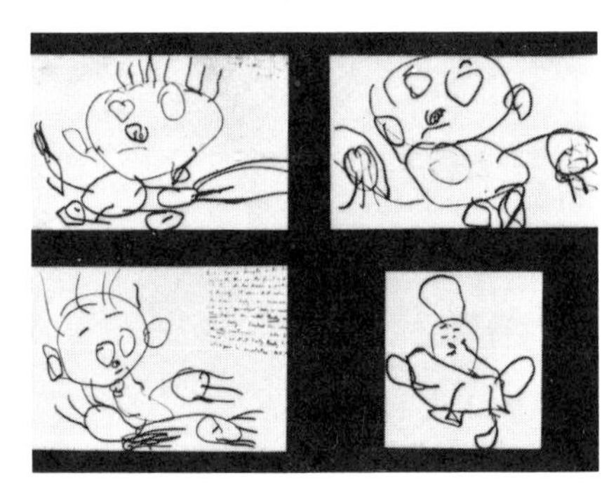

Shown at left is the first drawing Becky made in nursery school. She told her mother that **this** *is how all children drew. But at home, Becky made on the very same day a long series of figural drawings (right).*

ings are understandable, but aided by Becky's additional oral comments, the whole ambience of her school situation and her observation of it emerges.

Early Home Art

The contrast between the scribble made in school and the spontaneous drawings made at home tells something of Becky at school and at home. There is little of interest in the nursery school scribble, but her work at home is a rich revelation of her observations, her personal attitude in reporting her school experiences, and her startling ability to picture them. From the home pictures it is clear that Becky is unusually gifted and far more capable than the school situation brought out. The school experiences themselves were stimulating for only child Becky who enjoyed and observed the other children. However, the school climate evidently was a poor one for stimulating expression in drawing. Becky wanted to draw as the other children did. Only at home did her exuberance show itself in her drawings.

Three-year-old Claude arranged his man-figures in rows and enclosed them in a frame. In doing so, he created a primarily decorative order that indicated a premeditated design. The figures are the usual early efforts of a very young child to draw a man, just a head with legs. From this single picture, we might guess that Claude would go on for years drawing figures. On the contrary, different from other children, Claude produced stacks of mostly ornamental drawings and paintings, large and small, with elaborate details and carefully thought out technique, all conceived as aesthetic entities. There are few man-figures. Evidently these designs satisfied his aesthetic desire for something beautiful according to his own personal goal within the sheltered separate world he had created. Never having attended any preschool, he had developed by himself a highly formalized and patternized style of his very own. In kindergarten, he had been shown a number of techniques and had appreciated the know-how he acquired, the moreso since his teacher had not directed or forced him in any way. At home, he applied himself to whatever technique and media he had chosen as particularly adaptable to his nature and way of expression. For this unusually gifted child, kindergarten art was a stimulating learning experience. However, when he entered elementary school, his pattern of creating was disturbed. For weeks Claude was reluctant to attend class because art activities there limited his heretofor free, wide, and remarkable avenue of expression—to "potato-printing"! In second grade, his teacher tried to present more interesting problems. Claude recognized the teacher's efforts and repeated at home the "subject" assigned at school in an effort to improve his own drawing. But his attempts fell far behind his own self-initiated projects.

As different and single-minded in his drawings of engines, trains, trucks, and boats as Claude was in his pursuits, Benjamin entered nursery school in Canada toward the end of his fourth year. His travel experiences had widened his interests. He liked nursery school where he was given freedom to follow subjects of his choice and allowed to do them in his own style. His experiences in nursery school widened his outlook. They were of advantage to him because they did not conflict with his former interests and his inner world. The same thing happened in kindergarten and first grade.

In first grade, Benjamin drew a "Dinosaur (left)," a topic recurring inevitably in early grades. Being keenly interested in the modern machine world ever since he started making shapes, Benjamin drew at home a "Dinosaur" amidst present-day technology (right). The drawing technique at home and in school is the same.

Trenton also liked nursery school and had a very good teacher. The boy was fascinated by using a magnifying glass and a microscope to look at a bee's wing, a berry, and a leaf's veins. However, when he was then told to draw what he had seen, he was unable to do so. Other assigned subjects for drawing, a "mountain," "an egg," or "a pencil" also presented unsurmountable difficulties. They were not part of those internal images that prompted his need for expression in pictures. But, when he had a chance to draw his daddy or a house or anything of his own world, he was nearly as successful as in his home pictures, though a little more negligent or hurried. At home, he did long series of dragon pictures, houses, and family portraits. These satisfied his needs, while the picture work asked of him in school seemed to paralyse his usual ability.

Trenton was unequal to the task of drawing everyday objects like these at left. However, he made a picture (at right) of a painter who, for him, was a living and acting person. He drew him with the characteristics that he gave all his figures at that time, like the home drawing "House and Daddy" next to it.

The inner world from which each child views the outer world is his private window. What appeals to one child may have little interest for another. On the surface, a child's picture may seem of doubtful value, yet it is filled with tangible and intangible messages that tell much about his inner feelings, his perceptions, and outer relationships in his expanding consciousness.

Each child is different. Trenton, Valerie, Becky, Naomi, Rochelle, Benjamin, and others made quite early starts. However, the *pace of development,* conspicuous for example in Becky's case, *varied* greatly. Some children made their first humans early, others later. We cannot point out often enough that chronological age is of no importance whatsoever, that what one child draws at age four has no relevance to what another may draw at age three or even earlier. Becky reached a peak of productivity in number of drawings and expressiveness when barely two and one-half years old. Maya, on the other hand, drew understandably between three and one-half and four and one-half, but before and during this period she produced large numbers of paintings that seemed to proclaim her joy in color, shape, and the opportunity to work out her experiences. The same was true with Lori.

The *rate of production* also differed among our thirty children. Lori had periods of intense activity in which she produced several pieces of art in one day or a continuous flow during the month. At other times, her picturing was spaced further apart. Maya, with an almost unbelievable urgency to relive and express the experience of the story she had been told of her sister's birth, made thirty pictures of it in a single day. In contrast to her sister Carma's scant production of drawings, Maya made mountains of pictures.

The parents of Anne and John and Claude and Paul did not send their children to nursery school because they had observed their children's development at home and questioned whether school attendance might not interfere with it. In these cases, the parents' apprehension was confirmed later. Attending elementary school did cause a negative effect and their children did not meet with understanding by their teachers. Such gifted children as Cheri, Anne, or Claude received no recognition of their art achievements, which were ignored. Rochelle had happier experiences in nursery school and in her art sessions at church. Her teachers, aware of her trend in art expression, went along with it. Rochelle's drawings and paintings do not show much difference between school art and home art except that she seemed to give it more time at home. Maria, Maya, and Valerie did their art work less well in school, but this did not interfere with the higher quality and greater progress at home.

Rochelle's mother told of the opposite experience of her older son. Most of his drawings were made in school. The teacher deserves great credit for David M.'s art activities, although any interest in art he had at school or at home vanished when he was eight years old. Other activities had a

David M. had no interest in picture-making at home. The two color drawings at left were made in school, at ages four and one-half and five, at which latter age the figure in ink at right was drawn at home.

stronger claim on him. His mother was impressed by the teacher's ability to rouse her son's interest, since at home he showed indifference to art activity. One can speculate that, as a result, she later paid much attention to the home art of the younger sisters. She provided them with materials and showed great appreciation and pride in the girls' achievements.

The parents of our thirty children are not representative of parents in general in regard to their children's art. In this study, the group of parents are exceptional because their interest was strong enough to cooperate in the assembling of their children's work. Many of them noted down not only the dates and their children's comments, but frequently added their own observations or answered questions by the author. What they have done may be of help to other parents and to persons in charge of child centers and comparable facilities, whether as professionals or nonprofessionals.

Parents differ in their attitudes toward children's art activities. Many parents consider these activities a kind of play for which they must provide materials that constantly litter up their homes and end in the trashcan. They may find their small children's endeavors unintelligible and therefore believe them to be futile. Even intelligent, alert parents often pay attention only when the child has reached a point that "makes sense," which is seldom before the age of five. For example, the father of very gifted Cheri, whose accelerated development led her to draw with adult artistic skill before age nine, did not pay attention to her work until she was five. Often a child's early efforts to express himself by drawing may not be encouraged, may even be ignored. Many children never have an opportunity to freely put down their thoughts, perceptions, and feelings in drawings, paintings, or modelling.

A young child usually does not expect his parents to understand his play and play-world, though he may take it for granted that they do. Some parents may be pleased and amused by the young child's early scribbles and go along with his interests. Others may think it preferable that he play with other children rather than fuss with papers and messy paints. Some frankly want children to stay out of their way and the pressing daily activities and work of adults.

Once a child makes a picture, he wants to show it. He expects recognition and perhaps praise for his achievement, even though it looks like jumbled lines and smears. Most of all, he wants to share the sense of fulfillment that kindles in him a great joy, a kind of triumphant, even ecstatic feeling. He wants to share for a moment, perhaps just a few minutes, this testimony of his experience. At this moment, the attitude of the parents may vary greatly. They may show interest, bewilderment, or assumed understanding. Not many parents recognize the drawing for what it is—a building stone of their child's personality. If parents do preserve any of these childish productions, they usually do so selectively, according to their adult value judgments, keeping only what they consider the "good" ones. Sometimes they may preserve pieces they consider as unusual achievement compared with that of other children, or they see in their child's work a beginning with promise of possible advantage in later life. Another consideration may be the storing of childhood mementoes, like photos or school prizes, to strengthen family bonds.

Most parents of these thirty young children had one thing in common: interest in what their child was producing. Some parents were fascinated by the very first incomprehensible attempts; the attention of others was drawn to later expression that is more intelligible to adults. But all these parents showed belief in the usefulness and necessity of their children's assiduous attempts and encouraged them. They kept pictures even under stringent limitation of space. They demonstrated their pleasure by tacking the child's art product on the wall or framing what they liked best. They showed their pride in the child's work, and this acted as encouragement. Some parents were genuinely surprised that their child, on his own, had such ability. It was like a discovery they made and followed attentively. Obviously, parents can be instrumental in encouraging their children's efforts. At an age when verbal communication is still undeveloped, a child's art activities may be helpful for the study and understanding of him as an individual, but not sufficient for an appraisal of the individual's total development.

Tolerance of children's messes is an important matter. Trenton called one of his pictures "A Messer-Up." It was his judgment of the results of his effort, but also awareness of the disorder accompanying painting. Acceptance of natural though annoying disorder during children's work is a great factor in their productivity. The amusement of the parents, their "being with it," was sensed by most of these children and liked by them. Such a climate of encouragement helps to ease work habits gradually into a certain acceptable order. A paper carton may keep what the child cherishes and can put away himself. Valerie kept such a box under her bed, for no one but herself to touch. In it she rummaged eagerly to show *her* best-liked pieces.

Until their child's work is more advanced and has "meaning," many parents do not pay attention to it. Most often they keep and show the first human face or figure the child draws. Cheri's father said that he had not paid any attention until she was five, although as nearly as he could recall she was drawing "all the time." Despite the fact that painting is his avocation, he had not recognized her promising beginnings and therefore had not kept her earliest work. Later he encouraged her with great understanding and took her on his sketching trips.

A mother may praise an older child's superior pictures and be unable to see the merits of those of the younger child. Praise of one child's work, whether warranted or not, can prove discouraging to the other child who may stop his picturing activities. Fortunately this does not seem to happen frequently; the child's urge to express himself is stronger than anything else.

Some parents showed insight into the differences of character among their children. They understood the great differences in style and amount of pictorial production among them. They also were aware that one child may not want to do what brother or sister finds so absorbing. These parents offered encouragement to each child and avoided comparisons.

Some parents view their children's pictures mainly as measures for their intelligence, but they are unaware of what picture making means to the children themselves. They do not recognize the manner and extent in which their children's pictures indirectly represent a growth factor. They take little notice of comments that accompany the act of scribbling, comments that may be very illuminating, often surprising, and gainsay the first impression made by the drawing. Their appraisal and appreciation is, we might say, at the level of their own understanding.

A relatively large number of parents in this study were themselves interested in art, either professionally or as an avocation; a few were active in painting or crafts; others attended art courses; still others developed interest in art because of their children's art. Some of the parents sought information on child art by reading about child development or taking related courses. This was often helpful but it was also a temptation to try to apply too soon an as yet limited knowledge. In such instances they may compare children's achievements by age level and apply conclusions from their readings to their own child. They learn that children go through a series of developmental steps and watch whether their child follows those steps, whether he is "doing right," whether he differs from the "average." Sometimes they worry needlessly, forgetting how keenly they themselves are aware of the differences among their own children. One child enjoys scribbling, another playing with dough in the kitchen, another enacts his fantasies. They play differently and chances are they are finding something needed in their differences. One child's attempts may not be like another's, yet from the standpoint of *his* interest or *his* situations, his attempts may be quite as logical and natural as those of the others.

Of course it all depends on what, at this stage, is considered the "norm." Is chronological age or mental age a guideline or perhaps neither? Does one judge by the educational status of the parents or their way of life? Should one use an average that refers to the United States or to other nations such as Japan with its extraordinary child art?

Exposure to new situations can produce a wealth of experiences from which a child grows and develops. Entire patterns may follow, not only different from the expectations of adults but actually foreign and incomprehensible to adult outlook. Going for a walk, visiting the zoo, taking a trip, or moving to a different place of living are impressive experiences; they were recorded by many pictures of some of the children of this study. The impact may not show immediately, but may occupy the child's thought and imagination for a long time afterwards. David's interest in the family's moving far away widened his subject content and gave rise to strange pictorial combinations and later to delayed expressions of past experiences.

Children do not need to be constantly stimulated. They also need, and it is an important need, to be left to themselves. They can spend hours in contemplation, in exploration, discovery, and fantasy. Benjamin's small aquarium became for him the ocean itself. The house and family of Maya's friend Ann became, for a while, the center of her interest, and of Maya's development of house pictures, inside and outside. These houses served as a situational stage for her friend's people who lived there. Children need time to assimilate what they experience and then to expand it; they need time to dream, each child in his own way.

Some parents had kept their child's drawings from the first one on, noting the dates, writing down the child's comments and their own, and thus following and retaining a history of development that helped their own understanding. Becky's mother did this, as did Ananda's mother and several other young mothers in this study. Some children started "books" at a very early age, telling an entire series of events in their own manner. Catharine did so at age three. The children sometimes dictated to their parent additional explanations of the picture stories, as did Ananda or Jim. This cooperative effort gives both the parent and child a feeling of having accomplished something important to them. Some children in this study, for instance Becky or Carma, made "writing" lines on the pictures which, they said, told about the content, comments which some mothers wrote down elsewhere. Of course, what the very young child "writes" is undecipherable to the adult. Sometimes the child forgets his own story and possibly the meaning of the picture shortly after, yet it is an important step in communication and development of self.

The children of this study, because of their parents' cooperation and interest, which indeed made the study itself possible, enjoyed a favorable climate for early and continuing pictorial expression. The many series of drawings of these children on the same or similar subjects showed that they were involved in clarification or even solutions of their experiences, their observations, their sense perceptions, their relationships to other people. They had to verify and strengthen what happened in their lives and find their own place in relation to events. But they also wanted to advance their skills. Within this diversity of motivations, they developed as people.

Child art cannot be separated from the child's general development. The role of art in the development of the very young is yet to be satisfactorily described, although much more is known of child development. Child art is not a learned accomplishment such as addition or multiplication. We may regard the usefulness of child art in the light of what microbiologist René Dubos has to say: "Children who acquire a rich stock of perceptual patterns . . . *early in life** tend to have greater facility in building up the more complex patterns and labels required for conceptual thinking in later life."

*Italics by author.

For examples of school-related art as compared with that done at home, view MEDIAPAK 12, frames 1-36.

Module Fifteen

School, Teachers, Parents:

For several decades some colleges and universities have operated nursery schools. These provide faculty and students who are professionally focussed on very young children with an opportunity to observe how the very young behave, how they learn, and how they react to learning situations and techniques. Nursery schools and day care centers have become more numerous than they were in the past and accept younger children. They have been established for different reasons. Some parents believe in the advantages of their children's association with other children at very early ages under adequate supervision by trained persons. Others consider preschools as providing care for children whose mothers have to work or continue their studies. Working mothers find that these institutions offer not only a workday security for their children but also opportunity for experiences, self-expression, and group activities.

In the preschool, kindergarten, and earliest grades, children are usually given time for art activities. For those who had little art activity at home, the group activity often is stimulating. For those who had been quite active in art at home, the free quality of their home art may sometimes fade away. For some youngsters, the school environment seems to lead to conformity rather than to creativity. The rare talented child appears to go his own way. One of the children of this study definitely put aside her exceptional approach in an effort to do what others did and what the teacher wanted. One can see a wide range of effects of the school situation due, of course, to the fact that each child is different and will react in his own way.

The majority of the children of this study, some earlier, some later, attended nursery school and kindergarten before entering elementary school. They brought home their school art work. Their parents watched their children's work, offered comments, and asked questions. Many wondered why their child's work at school was different from that done at home. Some

Their Contribution to Childhood Art

found it less good. "Less good" seemed to mean two things: what parents considered less advanced than their home art and what to them seemed foreign to their children's interests or nature. Some parents more specifically noticed a lack of imagination in their children's school work. Several parents commented on school art being different from their child's home art, but that it did *not interfere with* his more creative, *spontaneous home art*. In some instances, the nursery school or kindergarten teacher showed understanding of the child's intentions and followed a laissez-faire policy, permitting free choice of subject and individual performance; school art and home art were much alike. Parents also could not understand why, during a period of less than a year, their child's work in school varied so much when compared to its developmental continuity at home. They wondered about teachers' different approaches and in some instances about school activities in art having a retarding effect.

The questions of these parents about their children's art experiences in nursery school or kindergarten, based on what these same children produced at home during the same period, raised a query about preschools.

Parents reasoned that their child had an opportunity to be with other children of comparable age, different from their younger or older siblings at home. He had the advantages of a trained person's attention during a manifold schedule of activities that offered learning situations, observations, and experiences different from those at home. The teacher, a nonparental authority, could make the child aware of things for which parents had neither time, opportunity, or background. Of course, although important on the pre-primary level, art is not the only consideration for schooling during these years. However, art activity is given time in preschool programs; it may open a field of discovery to young children and a means of self-expression to those who have no previous opportunity of picture making at home.

In most nursery schools, the child is offered a variety of art materials to help him toward self-discovery. This is, indeed, a field of healthy inquiry, stimulating his ingenuity. However, in the face of a very wide choice of materials, a very young child with little or no opportunity at home may be quite overcome. He may be hesitant at first, then may overreact to this challenging environment. Materials may take over. He may be unable to settle on some congenial medium to use for expressing his observations

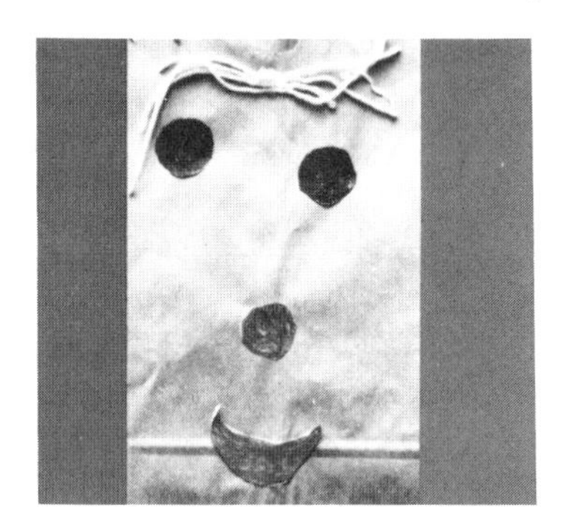

When she was three years, ten months old, Lori's "Face," pasted on a paperbag from ready-to-use paper pieces and string, was a popular nursery school "art" activity. However, the face's uniformity did not change or advance Lori's development of other faces drawn at this time and later.

and feelings. The distractingly rich variety of things to work with may result in impoverishment rather than fulfillment. Certain needs essential to the growth of his personality may not be met. Actually, the play with materials may become self-destructive. Even an observing and helpful teacher is seldom able to differentiate in the child's behavior between a reaction to the sheer novelty of the range of materials and a response which may incorporate new ways for nonverbal, visual communication.

In this study, parents provided materials for their children's home art activities, some even lavishly. Therefore, their children tried a fair array of media. Becky did best with feltpens; Benjamin and Maria used pen and ink, pencils, or color feltpens; Rochelle, Lori, and Maya could fulfill their own expectations more readily with paints. In their home art activities, these children confined themselves to a minimum of materials that seemed adequate to them, given time and encouragement.

In nursery school, these children were given papercuts, colorful papers, and various other materials to combine for "designs" or picture making. At home, they made use of the novel materials and skills they had learned about in nursery school or kindergarten, which their parents willingly provided. However, although the children took advantage of the media at their disposal and tried most of them at home, even the most skillful among them, like Claude, soon returned to their preferred medium of picturing and stayed with it.

Jennifer was given a great variety of media at home. She apparently was encouraged, if not directed, to use them. In fact, she had her own "nursery

Jennifer made this elaborate design from bits of material and other objects. In spaces between these, she drew a small face, scribbled ornaments, and made a frame in the shape of a heart. She dedicated the piece "to Daddy."

school" at home with its variety of facilities, all of which she used. To help her draw "difficult" subjects, she even was given outlines to fill in, dots and lines to connect such as those still used in some kindergarten or early elementary practice books. Jennifer performed neatly and skillfully, but might have gone further in developing her picture expression if left to her very personal, fastidious way of drawing the subjects that interested her.

Unless the teacher knows something of the child's interests and activities and of his personality *before* he enters school, she cannot very well estimate the child's needs for art expression *in* school.

For examples of the effects of school and home on child art and a variety of media and skills, view MEDIAPAK 12, frames 37-59.

(A) In this study, long periods of spontaneous art development at home by very young children have been described and documented showing their attitudes toward picturing. On the basis of this large amount of material and also of observation of children in school situations, we may rightly assume that *nursery schools can offer* fruitful, often *new and different fields of expression for the child.* For the parent, as well, the child's art experiences in nursery school may open new vistas.

For success in art activities of preschools, three major participants are involved and should be considered carefully. First and all-important is *the child.* What does he bring to school as an individual, living in a given environment to which he returns? What has been his experiential and developmental past? In which direction is he going?

Second, there are *the parents.* What is their attitude toward the school situation? Knowing their child as best they can, what do parents expect that he may gain by attending school at this very young age? What further insight can they gain themselves?

Third is *the teacher.* What is her attitude toward these very young children? What kind of knowledge or training does she have to guide her? To what degree does she recognize a child as a person already significantly shaped, in no way a blank to be patterned according to what the "average" child is expected to be and to do?

Becky is an unusual example of the havoc that may be wrought in a preschool situation that offers certain advantages but is unfavorable for pictorial expression and development. As an only child, Becky was very pleased with the companionship of other children. She herself showed this in her home drawings. She portrayed the contacts made in school, all things observed there and enjoyed, including the teacher. However, not only was she by far the youngest when she entered nursery school at twenty-nine months, she also was of superior intelligence and advanced general mental development. Furthermore, she was extraordinarily precocious in drawing. Perhaps Becky appreciated inordinately the companionship nursery school offered and obviously was aware that she must fit in as one of the group in order to enjoy it. Her superiority seemed to be especially pronounced in drawing; she therefore "adjusted" to the scribble stage of her companions. After about two months of adjusting, her own ability broke down and deteriorated. Many months later, she made a new start, but her pictures lacked their former animation and originality. Even so, they were on the same development level or more advanced than those of other four and five year olds. Her case presents an unfortunate combination of a child's precocious pictorial ability, virtually cut off by her sensing that conformity was necessary, and a great wish to please a teacher whose lack of knowledge or ineptitude kept her from recognizing a gifted child and helping to develop this gift. Although the influence one or more children exercise on other children also must be taken into account, this is on the whole of a general, behavioral nature. Becky is one exceptional case. At these very young ages, children do their art work side by side, pursuing their own thing. The author frequently has had occasion to observe the concentration of a child on his own subject and medium, even when his neighbor tried to show him how to go about it.

For examples from the special case of Becky, view MEDIAPAK 12, frames 60-82.

(B) What happens in the child-parent, child-school, and parent-school situations? These interactions form a complex network with differently situated centers that influence the interests and achievements of the individual child. Desirable results in preschooling come from a sensitive balance in these relationships.

The child himself and his art raise several questions. Is his art activity in school his first experience or has he previously drawn and painted at home? The teacher may want to find out first what the child's interests are. If he has done art at home, how much of it did he do? How absorbed is he in this activity? What, if anything, does he say during or afterwards about his work? Answers to such questions may provide some insight for the teacher. In fact, seeing the child's home work is valuable to her as an indicator of his "self" and therefore important to know. Who are the family members? Does the child have friends of the same age and, if so, does he tend to admire or envy, or cooperate or compete with his companions, or does he want to lead them? Is he absorbed in nature, interested in his mechanical surroundings, modern machines and vehicles? Is he verbal? Is his verbal expression an adjunct to his art expression or does it conflict with it? Do his home pictures indicate personal relations, response to sensory experiences, or point to specific observations and ideas? Does he act out vicariously on paper what he would like to do? Does he go about his art quite independently? What media and materials does his home provide? Are his parents' attitudes toward his art indifferent or a matter of interest, even preoccupation?

The parents, to some degree, also are teachers, though without a school; they may be aware of children's development in general and the steps of maturation involved. Do they evaluate their child in the light of such information, perhaps compare him with other children or brother and sister? Do they think of him as different and as an individual? Are they interested in knowing their child by way of his art? Do they look at it as one of many childish plays or appreciate his art as a meaningful activity? Do they encourage him? In other words, what are the parents' standards and how do they compare with those of the school? Do they compare his verbal ability with his pictorial expression? Do parents "learn" from their children and modify their behavior as a result? Are their expectations high in regard to the child's advances in his art, his perfecting of technique and skill, or have they a "wait and see" attitude?

The teacher in her way also represents a parent away from home. What resources does she have to act upon? Hopefully having studied the art of very young children and acquainted with great numbers of their work, the teacher will know about the overall similarity of childhood art. She may be aware of its distinctive characteristics and understand their place in art development. Will she perceive the child as an individual who may differ from his companions in maturity and ability as has been found and shown in this study? Can she see it in his art? With awareness of similarities and differences, the teacher will avoid comparisons of "good" or "bad," "advanced" or "behind"—comparisons that prove of little value for the child, apparent though they may be to the teacher.

There is endless variety in the way children do their art work. Some children are "tidy," others quite careless; one child's picture may seem "empty," the space barely used, another's spilling over with content; one will give the impression of movement, vivacity, action, another that of rigidity. The many hundred pictures shown here are but a part of the output of these thirty children. They attest to the differences in expression and presentation.

After a period of observation, the teacher may find that the medium the child is using does not fulfill his aim, is not adaptable to his technique of expression. She may be able to suggest that he try another medium. Crayons, for example, impede an accurate line technique, and are equally impracticable for color mixtures or brilliance. When a child has found a medium that works for him, he seems more able to picture what he has to say. He may explore other materials, but usually will return to his favorite. Similarly, he may have a favorite size. After a length of time, the long-used medium may no longer fulfill the child's aims and may be superseded by what seems a "better" one. Development may lead to different interests which then call for other media, techniques, and sizes.

The teacher also should observe the difference in time required by each child to finish to his satisfaction what he has started. Some children take a few minutes, others want to stay with their work a long time. This may be a difficult problem because of schedules or because the child who is given a longer time for his work may not wish to miss whatever other activity is afoot. At this very young age, an interruption may put a full stop to his work; it just may be not possible for him to return and continue in the same vein.

Another important matter for the teacher is her awareness of the young child's pursuit of *one* subject, *one* pattern, in the course of a large number of drawings, paintings, clay-forms or constructions that may look like just so many almost identical repetitions. Like Trenton with his "Dragons" or Paul with his "Boy-in-His-House," the very young child has a need to repeat himself, to be at home with his creations, comfortable with what he is doing before going on. This compulsion may be compared with the continuing use of certain words, games, gestures, or jumping exercises. One could describe them as long sequences of "self-competitions," whether exact or improved or even momentarily deteriorating. They appear to be necessary to the child's development.

The teacher promotes self-learning by not imposing ideas and judgments on the children's work. She guides them best when answering questions or offering help in understanding materials and matters of skill. She also learns from each child as she searches for meaning in his often puzzling creations. A child's early productions cannot be reasoned with. It is the rare teacher who develops in-depth understanding of young children's art expression.

The three-dimensionality of modeling, and that of building and constructing, appeals strongly to the very young child. In a school, this kind of representation can be more easily realized than at home. But the teacher or parent who considers gains in "learning" should remember that two-dimensional pictures must represent a three-dimensional world. Through drawing and painting, the very small child figures out a way to make himself clear by following his own peculiar concepts of picturing spatial situations in ways very different from the adult view. Among our thirty children, some already represented grouped situations at age three. They showed two or more persons and objects in a meaningful relationship.

Becky, Benjamin, and many other children had their own methods of implying space. Because adults are accustomed to an illusory, "photographic" presentation of depth or realistic paintings such as those of Andrew Wyeth, they have great difficulty in understanding the child's early representation of space. They cannot grasp the spatial situation in the child's picture, and many believe that so young a child is not aware of spatial arrangements. The very young draw from several viewpoints, combining those they can best represent. The child creates a space complex with elements in unexpected positions in relation to each other. When the adult tries to penetrate the meaning of the child's baffling picture, he must shake off his traditional way of looking and try to become familiar with certain rules that help him disentangle the elements or parts, even the directions, and thus he can possibly figure out what the child's placements imply.

The young child, as Luquet observed in 1913, forms an internal image of people, real objects, and creations of his imagination. These internal images are projected on his drawings and paintings and also guide his modelings and constructs. If another way of representation is offered or imposed, it is very confusing for the child. For instance, Becky drew her own "Thanksgiving Turkey." She made the bird in profile as most children's

The teacher drew a model of a turkey in front view and another one in side view as "keys" to help the children. Children draw birds in their more characteristic view, from the side, as Becky did here at home. For school, she failed in drawing the perplexing front view.

schemata are drawn, this being the most characteristic view of birds. Being an imaginative child, she drew her turkey in the open, under stars. In kindergarten, her teacher wished to assist the children in drawing this "difficult" subject by showing them *how*: a front view, uncharacteristic for the shape of any bird, and also a side view. Becky's own clear image became confused and her front view was a failure. Claude, at three, made a front view of a peacock. He did so because it conveyed fully the brilliant fan of spread-out plumage. But he gave his bird the front view he knew: a human face! Weeks ahead of Christmas, Becky drew innumerable trees on her own. From a primitive beginning, she developed the trees toward richness and glorification of the event. Shortly before the holiday the teacher, believing young children unable to draw trees of their own, passed out identical, cut-out green paper silhouettes of Christmas trees to be filled in with bits of paper and the like as decorations. Becky's work on these "prescribed" trees was poor and artificial, far below her own crea-

Becky made these two richly-decorated trees on the twentieth and twenty-second of December. One is placed outdoors under the sky. Becky must have been surprised to be given in school a pre-cut paper tree for making a Christmas tree picture after her experiences in creating her own trees.

tions. In this as in other cases, children were not helped; they were kept busy with ready-made mechanical operations in which imagination and thought, even skill, could not unfold.

The teacher may have a deep influence on children of this very young age if she shows her interest by suggestive questions that may start the child thinking. A child needs to be left to self-exploration, to trials of his own. Of course, he may also need some help in manipulating some materials or setting up work. Painting on large papers on walls or on easels initiated more than thirty years ago has disadvantages. Paints run down in streaks and drip, and most children are far too intent on what they want to say to bother about it or pay attention to advice on how to prevent these accidents. They will find out eventually. Now paints are available that do not drip. Large papers for painting are not a logical necessity; they are needed when wide brushes are used. Some children prefer smaller paper and finer brushes. With sufficient floor space or low tables to work on and nondrip paints, there is a better chance of success.

The home art of the very young showed the advantages of developing their own subjects. The techniques and media in which they presented them were individual and unique in regard to character of line or color. Benjamin invariably crowded his paper and chose moderate sizes. His drawings, based on form, were done in pencil or pen, black or colors. Lori, on the other hand, needed large areas because she mainly explored color paints. Paul, Catharine, and others frequently used very tiny spaces on which to draw. If one child is bent on tiny angular forms, another on big swinging loops or expanded areas, it seems that the nature of the child prescribes his technique. Why change it? Guiding them in an opposite direction may well impede their development. Children's art is not only based on things seen, but also on things felt and imagined, on wishes instead of facts; it is an extension of the child's ego. Individual differences are reflections of the self and indicate the need for the teacher's support of the child's own technique, not a contrary redirection. Help in choosing or reassurance in case of doubt may reduce, indeed pre-empt, the possibility of failures. Avoiding the trauma of failure is getting the child on his way.

A sympathetic attitude by the teacher and a genuine atmosphere of encouragement in school are necessary to the very young child away from home. He needs a bond with the teacher. Some children expect more than others, not only in reassurance that their work is "liked," but in *praise that shows understanding* of their work.

Cooperation with the parents will help teacher and child. The parent may profit by understanding the teacher's and the school's intentions. Parents who paid little attention to their young child's picturing before they entered school may now learn to see in them signs of their child's general development. Intangible as they may be, these gains are no less visible than more obvious progress from lesson-to-lesson in such concrete learning as reading and arithmetic later on.

Parents are delighted to hear a child singing to himself. They do not think immediately of a great voice that is developing, or a particular musical talent, but see the child's personal expression of well-being, of peace with himself and the world. Something similar occurs through the child's pictures. The process itself may be one of exploration of himself and the world, or a form of catharsis. Adults with little verbal facility who do not easily communicate with others often follow in thought a path similar to that of the very young child in drawing: they explore, weigh, and think over many things, either to come to a conclusion or simply to enlarge their outlook and knowledge of themselves. This may be noticed as a characteristic of a person; it is not questioned for being "good" or "bad." Why take a different attitude toward the very young child?

The teacher who can communicate with the child's parents is in a position to encourage them to foster art activity, to accept its value, to gain information for a better understanding. An exchange of observations on the child's home art and school art also is a further step to the child's advantage.

Some children are interested at an early age in writing and reading; they may have a fast verbal development. These are skills for which parents are particularly alert. What parents notice and what the teacher notices in school may be complementary or contradictory. Whatever it is, awareness, appreciation, encouragement are gains for the child and parent.

Art also is one of the important means by which the young child can externalize and communicate his learning experiences. A child's direction may be toward observation of insects, birds, or bats—as Claude's or Allan's were; the habits of mother and grandmother—as Becky and Jennifer so vividly demonstrated; or the great wonder at mechanistic miracles of our civilization—as Benjamin and David showed them. Catharine, Lori, and Paul reflected their joy in nature's phenomena—trees, sky, rain, fog, and clouds—while other children expressed their delight in stars, sun, and moon.

The multitude of questions raised in this chapter cannot all be answered satisfactorily. It is apparent that *no one method can* be effective for an entire group and at the same time *properly serve one child's situation* as it arises. Close observation of the child will reveal his inclinations, the course he wants to follow, and suggest the guidance that he needs. However, self-discipline and self-development are as fundamental as outside instruction. No course, no imposed lessons, no prescribed activities can fit an entire group for developing the riches, inherent but different, in each very young child.

Art is a vital tributary that feeds and enriches the great flow of a child's development. It helps make him a person who enjoys life and contributes to the lives of others. Art activities are directed toward the whole child.

Module Sixteen

Awareness of

Young children's experiences of what they feel to be beautiful are strong and often lasting. To them may apply a comment on art by the Russian poet and writer Boris Pasternak, that art is "something concentrated . . . a principle . . . *present in every work of art . . . a hidden,* secret *part of its content.*"* The small child thus responds to art, not conscious it is *art* that moves him.

During his earliest years, a child's world is ego-centered; most of his experiences and discoveries are entirely orientated to his self. Whatever awareness he has that might be termed aesthetic is expressed by the few words: "I like it" or "it is pretty." His awareness of anything remotely touching on "Art" is vague and must be related to his own life. If at all, it can be observed only in his play and responses to situations. He is involved solely with his personal experience of the outer world as far as he knows it and as far as it has to do with him.

A four-year-old boy, for instance, revisiting with his mother a place with which he had been enchanted the year before, did not recognize the grand view across the lake—nor the forest path leading to it—until he came to a big fir tree under which he stopped and exclaimed, surprise and wonder shining in his eyes, that this was where he had played; he proceeded to recognize, indeed greet and welcome, all the little rocks and plants and the huge low branches forming a roof over the spot. It was like a homecoming. He had not responded the year before to the view that inspired his parent and he did not do so now; but a very personal feeling was revived for this tiny bit of intimate world and the pleasant playground it had been. His "beauty spot in nature" came from a different approach than that of his parent.

*Italics by author.

Art in Life

An adult may have few indications of how a child is affected by an aesthetic experience. Little is expressed in words. After-effects of early episodes bathed in theatrical light and colors may survive in later life or occur in exaggerated flashes of memory. Later, some incident may call forth an astonishing revelation of the depth of the impact.

A three-year-old in a backwoods country entered a spacious but simple room, its wooden walls brightened by oil lamps, its floor warmed by colorful Indian rugs, and stopped, exclaiming emphatically, "This is *nice!*" The child was having a truly aesthetic experience. His own home, structurally not different from the one over which he exclaimed, was bare, simple, and crudely lighted. It seems quite clear that the child was caught by the intensity and impact of a familiar framework warmed by an artistic touch. Perhaps he had a vision of his own home, enriched by the actually modest things that appeared to delight him. This kind of experience opens the door to appreciation. It is within his own familiar world, yet in a way, is related to art.

When a four-year-old girl at the beach makes a sandy hollow for a pond, fills it with water, and puts her catch of baby catfish in it, this may only be curiosity, the wish to observe what these baby-fish will do. But when she then gathers leafy twigs and flowers, sticks them into the sand around her pond, collects pebbles for a border, traces a "walk" around it, puts decorations around her neck and in her hair, opens her paper umbrella, and then sits down decorously near the pond, she has "beautified" a whole scene and created an aesthetic ambiance. She has shown that she is conscious of a charm that can be added to a natural surrounding. She has satisfied an interest in nature and expressed aesthetic sensitivities. We can be sure that other emotions and feelings have been involved in making her beautiful pond. In their play activities, children frequently indulge in such engaging adornments of practical, nonartistic activities that adults seldom observe for what they are—an extra response to beauty in an art-in-life situation.

A small black boy, about six years old, took a streetcar every Saturday from his home in a ghetto district to the museum at the opposite end of the city. His fare was given him by an understanding museum curator who was teased by her associates who expected the boy to buy candy or ice cream with his carfare. However, the boy came regularly. It was noticed that he barely glanced at pictures or other works of art in the museum, not even the display of armor so attractive to the young. He appeared as a passive spectator in the midst of class activities. When asked about his museum visits, he said, "It's nice here. I like to walk around, especially in the court." The inside court he referred to was very light and airy with many plants and a fountain beneath its lofty skylight, but no "art." The court attracted the boy week after week. The spaciousness and light, the atmosphere of relaxation, must have seemed to him a fairyland of freedom and quiet. His enjoyment was not related to specific works of art, but was the experience of being in an atmosphere of quiet grace.

Works of art may have real relevance for a very young child's daily living experience. His knowledge of home life is usually a matter-of-fact recognition of what life is for him. However, seeing the familiar experience reflected in an artist's work may add a new dimension to his awareness and understanding. The part of nature to which he has access—a sunset or a starry night, those animals or plants he gets to know intimately, the countryside he is familiar with or dreams about, the city street that belongs to him—all make him wonder about the world and himself. It may all seem ordinary until the vision of the artist adds glamor that transforms his practical concepts and sets his imagination to work. That is what happened to a boy who, among a large number of pictures, chose van Gogh's sketch of his bedroom because "there is a bed in which it would be lovely to sleep."

Through self-initiated discovery and then through guidance by teacher, parent, or companion, the child is bound to add something valuable to his enjoyment of life and to the growth of his personality. He may be drawn to a single aspect that reflects his own preoccupation and feelings. We can thus understand a six-year old who came, to all appearances, from a neglected home environment, was attracted by a family portrait. It seemed quite clear that the appeal was not the portrait as art but that it showed a *family, the child's idea of a family:* a mother reading to her children in the evening. No doubt, the child would have liked to have this kind of family life. Perhaps the intimacy and the time spent by the mother with the children called forth an unconscious yearning. Looking at the scene, he experienced it vicariously. The work of art with its intensity of mood penetrated his feelings and gave rise and shape to a fantasy of something outside his own world. This picture was an art experience for the child.

Awareness of form and colors, sound and silence, rhythm, taste, smell, movement, and immobility contribute to receptivity to art. A child may be able to show more clearly in his own pictures, in song, in games, or in quasi-theatrical activities the happiness experienced than he or an adult can convey in words.

Young children's awareness of art in the life around them often can be observed and encouraged. At the market, a child with his mother or a group of nursery school children with their teacher may be made aware of the beauty of foods aside from their practical use, can be made aware of the pleasure in looking at arrangement, display of colors, experiences preliminary to and part of the enjoyment of eating. Appearance and taste of food go hand in hand. As a youngster pointed out while viewing a painting, "a table that is beautiful to have dinner on." Though practical necessities and lack of time make it difficult, shopping trips are opportunities for discovery and enjoyment. Rediscovering in paintings and photographs the everyday life around him reinforces in a child more fastidious and artistic experiences in life.

Playgrounds should be planned to provide attractive space to enhance the pleasure of play. Some playgrounds do this. Others are often stark in looks although they offer space and facilities not available at home. Children like things that are green and alive—trees, flowering plants, animals, birds and bird baths, and fountains. Children as young as age two like jungle gyms and swings and slides, those facilities offering the pleasures of climbing, of exhilarating fast motion. If the usual play equipment can be near trees, the child in the swing can imagine himself in the wilds, flying to the sky. If the slide can send the slider through a patch of woods, he may explore as well as exercise or feel the mood of a sense of growth. Under such conditions the playground is a land of imagination where the children climb a wooded hill, mount the stairs of a winding path, then sail blithely down through "thick" woods all around them. In some of today's playgrounds, artists cooperate with planners. They put in simplified forms for exercising, sparse in details but strong in contours and planes. This reinforces perceptions of touch or movement. Wood not only helps create a more natural setting but also emphasizes the feel of materials. The child is exposed to healthy activity while the environment provides space; nature and aesthetic forms promote unconscious learning experiences that sharpen perceptivity. Play, nature, and art combine in also appealing to a child's sensitivity, not only to his physical energies.

A child's awareness of art may be difficult to detect at an early age. It may not be expressed, therefore does not register with parents or teachers. Unable to observe its effect, the adult may doubt it exists. It is not anything the child can demonstrate to have "learned," like tying a shoelace or reciting numbers. It may be revealed by chance, in an unexpected manner. Lori showed her pride in knowing about numbers in her paintings of "Number Patterns;" they were shapes in colors, an aesthetic response. A young child like Claude may pay very close attention to the skill and technique displayed in works of art, much as talented older children do. This attention to and observation of the "how?" is a form of learning. It is a need recognized by the child to understand better what he himself is doing and to expand his own ability of expression. Attention to a work of art's technique does not interfere with his individual childhood style. What he gains in skill and through observation is a visible receptivity to art, expressed in different guise in his response to his environment, his own art work, and perhaps later in words.

Exposure to art may be desirable. It may stimulate awareness of art and cultivate discrimination and taste. Works of art in museums or in homes may be experienced by small children in their own way. Their everyday life experiences may become crystallized through art. Visits to exhibits can have some effect at a very early age but should be quite short. Adult and child look at art in a different spirit, with different expectations and attention. One should not forget that art plays the role of *illustration* in the life of the very young. He projects himself in varying degrees into it as if participating in a live situation.

Most children love to collect things: rocks, plants, insects, odd things. They treasure their collections, which are their own personal little "museums," the items to be looked at, savored, an intimate part of their lives.

If a child shows interest in a work of art, the adult frequently likes to direct his attention toward prominent qualities of color, line, arrangement, or other characteristics. The child's response, if any, may be hard to interpret. Any impact of art itself may remain obscure and therefore open to question of what effect the "art" actually had. It is, for one, different from what adults expect. The response may be delayed and full of surprise, but rewarding. Exposing a young child to reproductions may be good in itself for later visits to an art gallery or to sculptures in gardens because recognition gives children great satisfaction. The child's home, his own room, with not too many pieces, is a good viewing place; so is nursery school. Although the child's reactions may be based on non-art interests, he may sense some quality that strengthens and deepens his feelings, and this is caused by art.

Adults have tried to introduce children of school age or earlier to abstract art; they believe it to be akin to child art and that it may awaken a response to line, form, or composition without the distraction of a story-telling content. It seldom attracts a very young child. Any response, like Becky's reaction, is acutely negative. For children, interested mostly in factual or imagined events, as were Becky, Benjamin, or Maria, abstract art may be just a plain bore. Children like Claude and Paul who themselves leaned toward ornamental, nonrepresentative aspects in their own art may respond more positively.

The message of art must be rooted in children's lives and interests. Ways to arouse their interest in art will take into account all of their feelings:

love and security, even fear, curiosity, and a perceptive attitude in tune with their general development. The artist creates an aura around his subject and lifts it above the ordinary. This helps the child in his first steps toward appreciation of art. In fact this is a training ground for discrimination and taste.

Exposing the young child to art may help him to "see," may guide him toward artistic perception, may therefore be worthwhile,—a necessary part of his development. It cannot be tested. *It must be trusted.*

Module Seventeen

The Very Young Child's

GENERAL CONSIDERATIONS

What are the art materials the very young child can best use? What can he do with them? In learning about their use he is extending what his sensory experiences have taught him. He is actually inventing translations of direct sensory experiences into a communicable form with the help of limited media. He will use *all* his senses for what he has to say, but will say it through *one sense only* —the visual. However, when he models, builds, or constructs, he uses not only vision but also his sense of touch.

When a very young child tries to paint, he manipulates a brush and explores its stiffness or softness, the length of the bristles; he uses his eyes to understand its shape and his fingers to confirm that shape. He grasps it, moves it, and uses his kinesthetic sense to learn how to "brush" with it. He senses paints by sight, touch, perhaps by taste (beware of poisonous materials!), tests their fluidity and the relation of thickness or thinness in their application.

It is clear that a child must experience brush and paints first for their potentials so that he can relate them to the third material on which he applies them, the paper, cardboard, or wall! He may work with his fingers which are his "primitive" brushes or their extension, the real brushes. He will add awareness of sound made by the dip in the paint, the drip on the paper, and the sensation of his fingers as he moves over the surface on which he paints. These primal functions, the knowledge acquired by them, his thoughts and feelings, all combine in a very complex process. In it the young child explores his senses, learns about them, and tries to make use of his learning. Adults who plan his activities and provide materials must take these factors into account.

Art Materials

A child's spontaneous art activities always reflect his desire to learn about the world and himself. He is curious about everything:

colors and forms—what is visible

the rough and the smooth—what he touches

the sweet and the sour—what he smells and tastes

how a car sounds when it screeches to a halt

how wheels turn and how he can identify with their motion

how wind and rain feel to the touch

how to respond to waving grasses, to an insect's trembling antennae

In his art he will translate all these experiences into line and color, even the feeling of warmth and "benevolence" of the sun.

Adults have lost much of the ability fully to experience their senses. In this loss they have diminished their understanding of children's sensitivity to everything around them. Of course, the child is not necessarily dependent on art activities for learning about his senses. Through art, however, he can give early expression to his exploration of things in nature and man-made things; and through expression, he grows in understanding. He examines his surroundings for their importance to *his* activities. While the adult turns away in disgust or fear when he sees a centipede, the child gives it his undivided attention, unaffected by the adult's established values of good or bad, serviceable or useless, beautiful or ugly. Later, he unconsciously begins to adopt adult values. Because a child is alert to sense perceptions, he is sensitive to strange differentiations. He may be able to distinguish by smell his brother's shirt from his own—a feat which the adult cannot match—or identify a distant car by the sound of its engine. In watching children's sensitivity to sensory perceptions, teachers and parents can help children to express their awareness, enlarge it, and learn from it.

Working with art materials, the very young child translates into visible form his experiences of reality and imagination. He starts to evolve a technique for doing it that he will develop according to his imagination and judgment. The media therefore should fit his particular phase of physical and mental development so that he can be articulate in pictures. When the media are right, many children picture with truly unbelievable rapidity, as if their images were distinct and ready as, later on, are words. Hence, it is important that parents and teachers give him materials and tools he is able to manage for his individual approach.

The parent and the teacher are influenced by what *they* wish to see the child doing and by what *they* have learned an average child does at a given age. The temptation is great to put a large variety of media at the disposal of the very young child.

What does the child want to picture, to form in clay or dough, and how can he do it? The child must find out for himself. If he tries too many materials, he may lose the goal he has in mind. The materials and tools are only a means to an end, though important ones. What will he enjoy working with, what will help him do successfully what he wants to do—*this is the goal,* not what an adult might enjoy seeing him produce.

In choosing materials and tools for children to work with, parents and teachers may consider a variety of approaches. They must rule out the prospect of simply keeping the child busy, occupied, quiet. A busy child may give his parents time for their own affairs or the teacher an opportunity to turn to other matters. In keeping the child "happy," the adult may avoid confusing demands, but this solution is short-lived and of little value to the child.

The young child, curious about and intrigued by what he can do, will explore and try out *any* kind of material. He will see what he can do with it and, more important, *what he can say with it.* The question is whether the material is adaptable for best giving form to what he has in mind. An optimal result, what is called "Prägnanz" in Gestalt terms, may be achieved if the technique is suited to the purpose. We must ask: do the materials and tools at the child's disposal lend themselves to developing techniques that interpret his ideas? It seems that tools and materials are basic, not just for development in art but for the growth of expression of the personality of the child.

MATERIALS FOR HOME ART

The very young child has two principal means of picture communication: *line* and *color.* While he uses both, he may favor one over the other. If color is the more satisfying formulation for him, he will not only use it but strive to accomplish his purpose even when handicapped by an unsatisfactory medium like crayons. This is where guidance is called for. If line is more helpful for his aims, and he is eager to develop shapes by contours, he will do best with a pencil or pen. This study has shown that the contour- and line-conscious child seldom foregoes color, but color is brought out by way of colored lines or by filling in some areas with color. Again, here it is that the parent will see the trend. In any home these two potential directions can easily be satisfied.

The very young child can use pointed tools safely if some initial watchfulness is exercised. Unfortunately, crayons are the most popular drawing tool; they are available everywhere and are established, mainly through the schools. However, they are unsuitable for producing a precise outline. Moreover, crayons are brittle, smear, and their colors cannot be mixed at this young age.

Materials on which to use pencil, pen, or other line-producing tools is easily available: paper. All through this study it was evident that paper, whether small, medium, or large was used as it came to hand, even tiny scraps; when a child wanted to draw, he seized anything to serve his purpose. David made many of his travel pieces on lined paper, some torn from small notebooks. Other children made very surprising pictures on scraps probably taken from waste baskets, smoothed out, and used for their art. Discarded papers, one side covered with print, were used by Benjamin and several other children almost regularly. Sometimes a child even worked on the printside as Catharine did when she drew her "Singing People," quite undisturbed that printed parts infiltrated her pictures. At this age the child sees only what he has in mind and needs to say. This is of paramount significance to him. He seems unconcerned about the intruding background that is entirely disassociated from his picture. In fact, he sees what is important to him, dismissing all else.

Surprisingly, some quite young children can manage water colors, mix them, and paint with them. Of course, this kind of ability varies, but it is indicative of their love of colors, the pleasure of creating their own mixtures, and the care they take to avoid a "mess." Trenton did paint-scribbles with watercolors before he was two years old. Skill and representational development do not proceed necessarily at a parallel pace. In Trenton's case, his inclination turned toward linear forms, therefore he continued mainly with pen, pencil, or feltpens. His early ability in managing watercolors was not an indication of a lasting preference for painting.

All children enjoy painting at some time and to some degree. Maya and Lori went all out for paints and brushes. Benjamin was able to handle watercolors cleanly and with insight into their nature but used them only as a passing phase. Others who leaned strongly toward line tried out paints in the way they experimented with other media, and then returned to their favorite. Tempera paints and watercolors sometimes are difficult for the child to use independently and care for, while pencil, pen, or feltpens are always around and can be kept and used by him.

Cutting out with scissors is another kind of work children like and can do at home. Scissors *cut* contours that a pencil would delineate, though scissors are less easy to handle in achieving exactness. Some children first draw their pictures, then cut around them. Combining cut-outs and pasting them in some arrangement may lead to an imagined three-dimensionality, especially if their cut-out pieces are not flattened on the ground they are pasted on. However, most children are most satisfied with drawing and painting for their continuing needs.

Among the thirty children of this study, there was almost no modeling or building. Those who went to nursery school and kindergarten sometimes tried materials at home they had used in school. At home, Claude and Paul made considered choices of media they had been shown in kindergarten and developed them at home for their own purposes. They did so especially with blow-techniques. Even so, their use of them made up only a small part of their home art.

To enlarge the variety of media to an extent that parallels the variety available in preschool appears to the author specious and an unecessary burden for parents. Parents may then feel called upon to "help" because of the necessity of showing the child "how-to-do-it," which may lead to interference with the child's own intentions. Parents are a necessary *public* for a child's performance, not *participants.*

After observing the needs of children for home art and what they were able to accomplish with the materials they had, we can recommend that parents provide the following:

Drawing

Paper, white and colored, medium-sized, discards with one blank side.

Regular Pencils, if possible black and soft.

Color Pencils, not waxy, but those that leave distinct color traces without smearing. Claude and Paul used "Prismacolor" pencils. A few basic colors are sufficient though — these pencils are expensive.

Color Feltpens come in assortments; however, a modest variety is sufficent. For the child who has a color preference—and most children have, for example purple or pink—one should consider this preference and include it. At least two different sizes of "point," fine-point and medium, should be included.

Writing pens or a fine-point black pen. Many children like the hard point and the accuracy they are able to achieve with it on small sized paper.

Painting

Paper of different sizes according to the choice of brushes. Rolls of shelf paper or discarded ends of wall paper (use wrong side) are more economic.

Brushes of two or three different widths.

Paints of different kinds. *Poster paints* can be mixed in thick consistency that may prevent dripping or in a thinner consistency for finer brushes. They can be kept in glass jars. A discarded dinner plate or similar flatish container may be used by the child to try his mixtures. *Bentonite paint* (it does not run or drip), a clay-powder, can be mixed by an adult by adding it to twice the quantity of hot water. It should stand two or three days, stirred occasionally, and be used in small amounts with tempera color added according to desired color. Three to four basic colors are sufficient for a child's mixing experiments. However, the child must be shown how to clean his brush after mixing (rags for cleaning) in order to keep colors pure for further uses.

Fingerpaints. Bentonite mixes also make good fingerpaints, or one of several mixes can be made by the parent (such as one part flour, two parts water, pinch of salt, beaten smooth). The same amount of hot water added and the mixture then boiled (stir!) until clear, gives an amount which, when used with tempera colors added to it (three primary colors), can be used directly on paper or spread on a washable surface. In the latter case, a sheet of paper can be placed on it, smoothed over with light pressure of the hand, then detached: a print! Few of the children of this study made fingerpaintings at home. Their mothers helped with the material because of the interest in this technique aroused at school. This is equally true of modeling and building. The few children who did work of this kind at home did not continue it.

Watercolors are handled well by children as young as three or even less. Four to six cakes or a small watercolor box with two sizes of brushes will do. Cakes must be pasted to a base or on a flatish utensil (shallow baking pan), and two glasses of water should be provided on the base or separately: one for mixing colors and one for cleansing brushes each time a new colormix is used. Rags for wiping brushes should also be provided.

Cut-Outs

Paper. Strong, colored papers are needed. Do not buy ready-cut shapes such as rounds, ovals, or squares; The child should do it himself. Further needed are paste and small scissors (provide blunted points for very young children under three or four).

Modeling

Real Dough, when mother bakes, is a great pleasure for children who then see their products baked.

Playdough or Plasticine can be worked with scissors, shaped with various blunt instruments, and patterns incised on them. Clay and models must be covered with moist cloth to prevent drying and crumbling.

Protection of floors, furniture, and clothes call for the use of newspapers indoors and outdoors, as well as aprons, rags for instant clean-ups, etc.

MATERIALS FOR ART IN SCHOOLS

Schools are obviously in a position to provide a greater variety of materials and media than can be offered at home. If the teacher's philosophy is that the school situation should stimulate the child's curiosity in directions different from what he does at home, the materials provided by the school can be many. The teacher, aware that children at home are intent on expressing their perceptions, experiences, thoughts, and feelings in an individual manner, will consider the circumstances. The approach may be that of letting the child lead the way; he may continue with media and materials that he has learned to handle at home, thereby maintaining the development acquired at home, but with a different audience and a different kind of encouragement, appreciation, and suggestions. This method worked with Rochelle and Benjamin. On the other hand, the teacher may infuse new ideas to be expressed by media different from those at home. These ideas may be transitory, the interest in particular media may be of short duration, but the child may feel the impact and adopt new media for home trials. Claude did so in kindergarten in a limited way; a few other children also made sporadic home trials of what they had learned in school.

Schools and preschools emphasize learning, but too great a variety of choice may be contrary to progress. In art instruction, learning may emphasize the medium and the skill to manipulate it. In emphasizing skill and manipulation, it may be forgotten that skill, like language, is a means of serving other ends. To communicate in language it is necessary to acquire a vocabulary and to use words correctly. To communicate through art, the child must find symbols (frequently not comprehensible to adults) that help him express what is "on his mind." His art language is in images. The child who speaks to himself and to others through art has to find his medium of expression and develop its use. In using it, he advances his own development, reveals his growing knowledge of self and others, and gives expression to his inner images, which are not only constructs of the mind but also a complex of sensory experiences.

Preschool and kindergarten may open a new means of expression to children who have never drawn or painted at home. For these children, a great variety of materials may lead to bewildering difficulties of choice. They may look upon materials as play to be tried and thrown aside. Manipulation may become the ultimate goal with little accomplished toward the development of expression. For the growth of their personalities, choice in materials must be made with forethought, that is, with the teacher being aware that sufficient time must be dedicated to any new experience.

To promote art activities in school surroundings, a sufficiently large, separate corner should be provided to secure a measure of privacy. There is also a great advantage in a schedule that is flexible enough to allow a child to "do art" when he feels like it. Of course, children may have to follow a schedule. Art activities may have a specific time allocation, but the spontaneity of the creative impulse has its advantages. Art activities can greatly aid the child's search for understanding himself and his world. The more self-initiated such activities can be, the more active will be an "in depth" exploration fundamental to individual development.

A physically well-organized arrangement of materials is desirable. Some materials, just as books, should be easily accessible: the child, then, can help himself. Other materials need to be stored in such a way that the teacher can give the child the green light to go ahead and work with them.

Drawing and painting promote thinking and reflection and exercise of the imagination. They lead to expression in symbols and make-believe. Modeling and constructs may promote learning related to the practical perception of textures, space relations, and motion. As the child's discrimination grows, his sensory perceptivity becomes more refined. Through observation he learns about textures, the impermanence of building with sand, the plyability of playdough, or the permanence of wood. In turn, the child learns to choose a material that fits his aim; he even transfers this knowledge to technique in picture making.

Where there is an opportunity for partly sheltered outdoor space, outdoor artwork may be welcome. Moreover, paved spaces, walls, and fences permit direct work on their surfaces with materials that can be cleaned off.

The purpose of this discussion is to provide information about the "natural" art development of the preschool child, his spontaneous home art in its growth and changes. The insight gained by following periods of art activities of the thirty children has led the author to consider pictorial expression to be particularly helpful in acquiring and using perceptual resources and in forming concepts. In these earliest years, expression in images seems to be a necessary companion to language development. Therefore, the author believes that drawing and painting, any manner of expression through pictures, is the most important single factor among the child's art activities.

According to the resources available to a school and the teacher (and aide)-to-child ratio, the materials listed below may be sufficient to stimulate and satisfy inventiveness and creativity of preschoolers. Materials described for the home use are also recommended for schools, but in larger assortments of color both for drawing and painting purposes; a greater variety of tools is also needed.

Drawing

Papers of many shades of color and all sizes and strengths.

Color pencils in large assortments.

Feltpens with great variety of point-sizes or width: round and square.

Avoid Crayons!

Painting

Bentonite mixes with a variety of color pigments, low tables, easels, etc.

Fingerpaints from a variety of different recipes (see bibliography).

Modeling

Clay can be used because it can be fired. At preschool ages, the manipulation of dough and clay may be primary factors; the child will fashion these materials like flat pictures. Modeling will play a larger role in school than at home.

Constructions and Building

Materials such as wood or metal scraps (the latter polished or to be handled with gloves) can be easily available from a carpenter or other workshops; also needed are nails, hammers, glue. Heavy paper or cartons, available from stores or storehouses, are a help for building and, in addition, their surfaces can be painted.

Any school will have some indoor and outdoor space to put up a clothesline to hang paintings for drying and for storing for a short time.

In conclusion, a great variety of materials is less necessary than a few well-selected media used within a schedule that permits the child to take time and be undisturbed in his work.

Related Readings

Some of the books and articles here listed may prove stimulating for a reappraisal of the role of young children's art, while others have only a tenuous relation to the present study and its findings. Unfortunately, the main questions asked by most writers are not *why* very young children express themselves through drawing but *how* their drawings develop toward an adult performance.

Few long-term investigations have been made and very few are home-centered. Most approaches are through school observations and use school-designed experiments. Translations of some publications in foreign languages or parts of them (French and German) would be helpful for teachers and parents for further information; researchers would avoid duplications of earlier experiments.

Wherever possible, the nature of the publication is marked with one or more identifying letters given below.

AE Art education
CA Children's art in general
DA Course of development of child art
G General content including child art
IA An individual child's art (according to Luquet: "a long term method that brings continuing results regarding an individual child's art which may not represent an average . . .")
IPs Psychological study of an individual child, including his art
ISC Several studies of individual children's art
M Many children (also statistical evaluations, according to Luquet: "the statistical method gives results of an 'average' which is only valid for the single event of the experiment . . .")
Mat Information about material and media
PA Personality and child art

PC Particular characteristics in child art
Pr Precocious development
Ps Psychological interpretation of child art
Sp Spontaneous art of children
Th Therapeutical approach through child art
VY *Very* young children (as early as scribble age)

BOOKS

Almy, M. *The Early Childhood Educator at Work.* New York: McGraw-Hill, Inc., 1975. *G, M, PC.*

Alschuler, R. H. and LaBerta W. Hattwick, *Painting and Personality.* Chicago: University of Chicago Press, 1947, 1970. *ISC, M, PA, Ps.*

Arnheim, R. *Art and Visual Perception: A Psychology of the Creative Eye.* Berkeley: University of California Press, 1960. *DA, PC, Ps, VY.*

Beck, W. *Self-Development in Drawing, as Interpreted by the Genius of Romano Dazzi.* New York: Putnam's Sons, Knickerbocker Press, 1928. *IA.*

Bland, J. C. *Art of the Young Child, Understanding and Encouraging Creative Growth in Children Three to Five.* New York: The Museum of Modern Art and New York Graphic Society Ltd., 1968. *AE, ISC, Mat, PC.*

Boutonier, J. *Les Dessins des Enfants* [Children's drawings]. Paris: Editions du Scarabée, 1953. *DA, PA, PC, Ps, Sp, Th, VY.*

Britsch, G. *Theorie der bildenden Kunst* [A theory of the fine arts], 2nd ed. Egon Kornmann (ed.). Munich: Bruckmann, 1930. *G.*

Di Leo, J. H. *Young Children and their Drawings.* New York: Brunner/Mazel, Inc., 1970. *ISC, PA, Ps, Th, VY.*

Dubos, R. *So Human an Animal.* New York: Charles Scribner's Sons, 1968. *G.*

Eisner, E. W. *Educating Artistic Vision.* New York: MacMillan, 1972. *AE, CA.*

Eng, H. *The Psychology of Children's Drawings: From the First Stroke to the Colored Drawing.* London: Kegan Paul, Trench, Trubner & Co., 1931. *DA, IA, VY.*

Fein, S. *Heidi's Horse.* P. O. Box 2303, Pleasant Hill, California, 94523, 1976. *IA, PA.*

Gaitskell, C. D. and M. Gaitskell. *Art Education in the Kindergarten.* Chas. A. Bennett Co., 1952. *AE, M, Mat.*

Gaitskell, C. D. and A. Hurwitz, *Children and Their Art.* New York: Harcourt, 1970. *AE, DA, M, Mat.*

Gesell, A. *The First Five Years of Life.* New York: Harper & Row, 1940. *G, M.*

Gould, R. *Child Studies through Fantasy: Cognitive-Affective Patterns in Development.* New York: Quadrangle Books, 1972.

Grötzinger, W. *Scribbling, Drawing, Painting: The Early Forms of the Child's Pictorial Creativeness.* New York: Frederick A. Praeger, Inc., 1955. *PC, Ps, VY.*

Harris, D. B. *Children's Drawings as Measures of Intellectual Maturity: A Revision and Extension of the Goodenough Draw-a-Man Test.* New York: Harcourt, Brace and World, 1963. *DA, M, PC, Pr.*

Hartlaub, G. F. *Der Genius im Kinde* [The child's ingenuity]. Breslau: Ferdinand Hirt, 1930. *CA, DA, PA, PC, Pr, Ps, Sp.*

Hildreth, G. *The Child's Mind in Evolution.* New York: King's Crown Press, 1941. *IA, PC, Pr, VY.*

Illich, I. *Deschooling Society.* New York: Harper and Row, 1972. *G, AE.*

Kellogg, R. *Analyzing Children's Art.* Palo Alto, Calif.: National Press, 1969. *DA, M, PC, Ps, VY.*

Krötzsch, W. *Rhythmus und Form in der freien Kinderzeichnung* [Rhythm and form in children's spontaneous drawings]. Leipzig: Haase, 1917. *PC, Ps, VY.*

Lark-Horovitz, B., H. Lewis, and M. Luca. *Understanding Children's Art for Better Teaching*, 2nd ed. Columbus, Ohio: Charles E. Merrill, 1973. *AE, DA, M, Mat, PA, Pr, Sp.*

Landreth, C. *Preschool Learning and Teaching.* New York: Harper & Row, 1972. *AE, G, Mat, VY.*

Landreth, C. *Early Childhood: Behavior and Learning.* New York: Knopf, 1967. *G.*

Lascaris, P. A. *L'Education Esthetique de l'Enfant* [Aesthetic education of the child]. Paris: Alcan, 1928. *G, PA, VY.*

Levinstein, S. *Untersuchungen über das Zeichnen des Kindes* [Investigating children's drawings]. Leipzig: R. Voigtländer, 1905. *CA, DA, M, PC, VY.*

Lowenfeld, V. and W. L. Brittain. *Creative and Mental Growth*, 4th ed. New York: Macmillan, 1970. *PA, PC, Ps.*

Luquet, G.-H. *Les Dessins d'un Enfant* [A child's drawings]. Paris: Alcan, 1913. *IA, PA, PC.*

Luquet, G.-H. *Le Dessin Enfantin* [Drawings by children]. Paris: Alcan, 1927. *DA, ISC, M, PC, Ps.*

Mendelowitz, D. M. *Children Are Artists, An Introduction to Children's Art for Teachers and Parents.* Stanford, Calif.: Stanford University Press, 1953, 1963. *CA, DA, ISC, M, PA, Pr, Sp.*

Pescioli, I. *Com'era l'Aqua* [When the floods came]. Florence: La Nuova Italia, 1967. *PA, PC, Sp, Th.*

Pfleiderer, W. *Die Geburt des Bildes* [Birth of a picture]. Stuttgart: Julius Hoffman, 1930. *CA, PA, PC, Pr, Sp, VY.*

Piaget, J. *Science of Education and the Psychology of the Child.* New York: Orion Press, 1970. *G.*

Read, K. H. *The Nursery School—Human Relationships and Learning.* Philadelphia: W. B. Saunders Company, 1976. *G, CA, PC, Mat, VY.*

Ricci, C. *L'Arte dei Bambini* [Children's art]. Bologna: N. Zanichelli, 1887. *M, PC, PS, Sp.*

Rodman, S. *Conversations with Artists.* New York: Capricorn Books, 1961. *AE*

Rouma, G. *Le Language Graphique de l'Enfant* [The child's graphic language]. Brussels: Misch and Thron, 1913. *CA, DA, M, PC, Sp. Th.*

Scupin, E. and G. Scupin. *Bubi im 4. bis 6. Lebensjahr* [Bubi during age four to six]. Leipzig: Grieben, 1910. *IA, PA, PC, Ps, Sp, VY.*

Weber, L. *The English Infant School and Informal Education.* New York: Prentice-Hall, 1971. *G, VY.*

White, B. L. *The First Three Years of Life.* Englewood Cliffs, N. J., Prentice-Hall, 1975. *G, VY.*

Winnicott, D. W. *Therapeutic Consultations in Child Psychiatry.* New York: Basic Books, 1971. *Th.*

Wolff, W. *The Personality of the Preschool Child: The Child's Search for His Self.* New York: Grune and Stratton, 1946. *PA, Ps, VY.*

Wulff, O. *Die Kunst des Kindes* [The art of the child]. Stuttgart: Ferdinand Enke, 1927. *DA, IA, ISC, PA, M, VY.*

Zesbaugh, H. A. *Children's Drawings of the Human Figure.* Chicago: University of Chicago Press, 1934. *DA, PC.*

ARTICLES

Ames, L. B. "Free Drawing and Completion Drawing: A Comparative Study of Pre-School Children." *Journal of Genetic Psychology* 66 (1945): 161–65. *PC.*

Alexander, C. "The Origin of Creative Power in Children," in *Art for the Preprimary Child,* H. P. Lewis (ed.). Washington, D. C.: National Art Education Association (1972), 32–49. *DA, PA, PC, Ps, VY.*

Alper, T. G., H. T. Blaine, and B. K. Abrams. "Reactions of Middle and Lower Class Children to Finger paints as a Function of Class Differences in Child-Training Practices." *Journal of Abnormal and Social Psychology* 51 (1955), 439–48. *PA.*

Arnold, L. R. "A Study of Aspects of Art Education for Four-Year-Old Children." Unpublished Master's Thesis, Florida State University, Tallahasee (1963). *AE, VY.*

Ballard, P. B. "What London Children Like to Draw." *Journal of Experimental Pedagogy* 1, nr. 3 (1912). *CA, M, PC.*

Barnes, E. "A Study of Children's Drawings." *Pedagogical Seminary* 2 (1893): 451–63; and *Studies in Education* 2 (1902): 109–12. *ISC, Ps, Sp. VY.*

Bried, C. "Le dessin de l'enfant: premières représentations humaines" [The child's drawing: first representations of humans]. Enfance 3, nos. 3 and 4 (1950): 256–75. *M, PC, VY.*

Brittain, W. L. "Some Exploratory Studies of the Art of Preschool Children." *Studies in Art Education* 10, no. 3 (1969): 14–24. *DA, PA, PC, VY.*

Brittain, W. L. "Research on the Art of Young Children," in *Art for the Preprimary Child,* H. P. Lewis (ed.). Washington, D. C.: National Art Education Association (1972): 18–31. *PA, PC, Ps, Sp, VY.*

Brown, E. E. "Notes on Children's Drawings." *University of California Publications in Education* 2 (1897): 1–75. *DA, ISC, VY.*

Bruner, J. "The Cognitive Consequences of Early Sensory Deprivation." *Psychosomatic Medicine, Harvard Educational Review* 29 (April 1959). *PA.*

Burckhardt, H. "Veränderungen der Raumlage in Kinderzeichnungen" [Changes of spatial position in children's drawings]. *Zeitschrift für paedagogische Psychologie* 26 (1925): 352–71. *PC.*

Cameron, N. "Individual and Social Factors in the Development of Graphic Symbolization." *Journal of Psychology* 5 (1938): 165–84. *PA, VY.*

Cižek, F. "Die Organisation und die kunstpaedagogischen Probleme des Jugendkurses" [Organization and problems of the children's art course]. Spezialvortrag, *4. Internationaler Kongress für Kunstunterricht, Zeichnen und angewandte Kunst,* Hauptbericht, Dresden (1912): 466-76. *CA, PC, Pr, Sp.*

Child, I. L. "Personal Preference as an Expression of Esthetic Sensitivity." *Journal of Personality* 30 (1962): 496–512. *PA.*

Douglas, N. J. and J. B. Schwartz. "Increasing Awareness of Art Ideas of Young Children through Guided Experiences with Ceramics." *Studies in Art Education* 8, no. 2 (1967): 2–9. *PC.*

Douglas, N. J. "A Study of the Easel Paintings of Kindergarten, First- and Second-grade Children in Directed and Free Choice Activities." Unpublished doctoral dissertation, *Florida State University* (1959). *PC, VY.*

Dubin, E. R. "The Effects of Training on the Tempo of Development of Graphic Representation in Preschool Children." *Journal of Experimental Education* 15 (1946): 166–73. *DA, VY.*

Engel, P. "Uber die teilinhaltlichr Betrachtung von Farbe unf Form im vorschulpflichtigen Kindesalter" [Observation of color and form content by preschool children]. Zeitschrift für paedagogische Psychologie und Jugendkunde 36 (1935): 202–14, 241–51. *PC, VY.*

Eisner, E. W. "Curriculum Making for the Wee Folk: Stanford University's Kettering Project." *Studies in Art Education* 9, no. 3 (1968): 45–56. *AE, CA, DA.*

Franklin, M. B. "Non-Verbal Representation in Young Children." *Young Children* (Nov. 1973): 33–53. *PC.*

Gesell, A. and L. B. Ames. "The Development of Directionality in Drawing." *Journal of Genetic Psychology* 68 (1946): 45–61. *PC, VY.*

Gibson, J. J. and P. M. Yonas. "A New Theory of Scribbling and Drawing in Children." *Cornell University, E D O* 17324 (1970). *PC, Ps, VY.*

Ghesquière-Dierickx, B. "Comment dessinent les enfants: Evolution du dessin seldon l'âge [How children draw: chronological development of drawing]. *Enfance* 11 (1961): 179–82. *DA, PA, Pr.*

Grosser, H. and W. Stern. "Das freie Zeichnen und Formen des Kindes" [Free drawing and modeling of the child]. in *Abhandlungen der Zeitschrift für angewandte Psychologie* (1913). Leipzig: Ambrosius Barth. *DA, ISC, M, PA, PC, Ps, Sp, VY.*

Grossman, M. "Perceptual Style, Creativity and Various Drawing Abilities." *Studies in Art Education* 11, no. 2 (1970): 48–54. *PA, Ps.*

Guillaumin, J. "Quelques faits et quelques reflexions a propos de l'orientation des profiles humains dans les dessins d'enfants" [Some facts and thoughts regarding the direction of profiles in children's drawings]. *Enfance* 14, no. 1 (1961): 57–75. *PC.*

Hanfmann, E. "Some Experiments on Spatial Position as a Factor in Children's Perception and Reproduction of Simple Figures." *Psychologische Forschung* 17 (1933): 310–29. *PC.*

Harms, T. "Presenting Materials Effectively" in *Art for the Preprimary Child,* H. P. Lewis (ed.). Washington, D. C.: National Art Education Association (1972): 92–109. *Mat, VY.*

Jacobi, J. "The Ego and the Self in Children's Drawings." *Die Schweizerische Zeitschrift für Psychologie und ihre Anwendungen* 12, part 1 (1953). *Ps.*

Kerr, M. "Children's Drawings of Houses." *British Journal of Medical Psychology* 16 (1937): 206–18. *PC.*

Lansing, K. M. "The Research of Jean Piaget and Its Implications for Art Education in the Elementary School." *Studies in Art Education* 7, no. 2 (1966): 33–42. *AE, G.*

Leroy, A. "Représentation de la perspective dans les dessins d'enfants" [Perspective in children's drawings]. *Enfance* 4, no. 4 (1951): 286–307. *PC.*

Lord, L. "The Role of the Teacher" in *Art for the Pre-primary Child,* H. P. Lewis (ed.). Washington, D. C.: National Art Education Association (1972): 58–73. *AE, VY.*

Lukens, T. "A Study of Children's Drawings in the Early Years." *Pedagogical Seminary* 4 (1896-97): 79–110. *DA, VY.*

Luquet, G-H. "La narration graphique chez l'enfant" [The child's graphic language]. *Journal de Psychologie* 21 (1924): 183–218. *PC, Ps, Sp.*

Luquet, G-H. "Le réalisme intellectuel dans l'art primitif: I. Figuration de l'invisible; II. Le rendu du visible" [Realistic meaning in primitive art: I. Representation of the invisible; II. Representation of the visible]. *Journal de Psychologie* 24 (1927): 765–97, 888–927. *PC.*

Madeja, S. S. "Early Education in the Visual Arts" in *Art for the Preprimary Child,* H. P. Lewis (ed.). Washington, D. C.: National Art Education Association (1972): 110–27. *AE, VY.*

Maitland, L. M. "What Children Draw to Please Themselves." *The Inland Educator* 1 (1895): 77–81. *DA, M.*

McBroom, P. "Mining the Child's Art." *Science News* 93, no. 4 (1968). *CA.*

McVickar, P. "The Role of the Parent" in *Art for the Preprimary Child,* H. P. Lewis (ed.). Washington, D. C.: National Art Education Association (1972): 50–57. *AE, VY.*

Partridge, L. "Children's Drawings of Men and Women." Studies in Education 11, no. 5 (1902). *DA, M, PC.*

Perryman, L. "The Young Child in His World" in *Art for the Preprimary Child,* H. P. Lewis (ed.). Washington, D. C.: National Art Education Association (1972): 6–17. *PA, VY.*

Piaget, J. "Perceptual and Cognitive (or Operational) Structures in the Development of Space in the Child." *Acta Psychologica* 11 (1955): 41–46. *G, PC.*

Piaget, J. "L'explication de l'ombre chez l'enfant" [The child's concept of the shadow]. *Journal de Psychologie* 24 (1927): 230–42. *PC, VY.*

Pines, M. "A Child's Mind is Shaped Before Age Two." *Life* (Dec. 17, 1971): 63–68. *VY.*

Porot, M. "Le dessin de la famille: Exploration par le dessin de la situation de l'enfant dans sa famille" [Drawing his family: the child's position within it as seen in his drawings]. *Pédiatrie* 41, no. 3 (1952): 359–81. *PA, Th.*

Read, H. "Art As a Unifying Principle in Education" in *Child art: The Beginnings of Self-Affirmation.* Conference at the University of California, 1966. Berkeley: Diablo Press (1966): 17–41. *G.*

Salome, R. A. "A Comparative Analysis of Kindergarten Children's Drawings in Crayon and Colored Pencil." *Studies in Art Education* 8, no. 2 (1967): 21–28. *Mat, VY.*

Schaefer-Simmern, H. "The Mental Foundation of Art Education in Childhood" in *Child Art: The Beginnings of Self-Affirmation.* Conference at the University of California, 1966. Berkeley: Diablo Press (1966): 46–68. *AE, ISC, PC.*

Sears, P. S. and Dowley, E. M. "Research on Teaching in the Nursery School," in *Handbook of Research in Teaching,* N. L. Gage (ed.). Chicago: Rand McNally (1963). *AE, VY.*

Speed, W. J. "Early Expressionists." *Film News* 24, no. 1 (1967). *PC.*

Stern, W. "Die Entwicklung de Raumwahrnehmung in der ersten Kindheit" [Perception of space in earliest childhood]. *Zeitschrift für angewandte Psychologie* 3 (1909): 412–23. *PC, VY.*

Stern, W. "Uber verlagerte Raumformen" [Displacement of three-dimensional shapes]. *Zeitschrift für angewandte Psychologie* (1909): 498–526. *PC.*

Stern, C. and W. Stern. "Die zeichnerische Entwicklung eines Knaben vom 4. bis zum 7. Jahr" [Drawing development of a boy from age 4 to age 7]. *Zeitschrift für angewandte Psychologie* 3 (1909-10). *IA, ISC, PA, PC, Sp, VY.*

Tezner, O. "Das Wunderkindphänomen in der Entwicklung des normalen Kindes" [The prodigy and the development of the normal child]. *Zeitschrift für Kinderpsychiatrie* 18 (1951): 257–66. *DA, Pr.*

Wiedhaber, R. "Introduction to Swiss Folk Art." Pro Helvetia Foundation (1968): 9–11.

Wintsch, J. "Le dessin comme témoin du développement mental" [Drawing, testimony of mental development]. *Zeitschrift für Kinderpsychiatrie* 2, no. 3 (1935): 33–44, 69–83. *DA, PA, PC, Ps, VY.*

Young, E. "Art in Children's Learning" in *Art for the Preprimary Child,* H. P. Lewis (ed.). Washington, D. C.: National Art Education Association (1972): 74–91. *AE, VY.*

Age Range of Thirty Children During Participation in Study

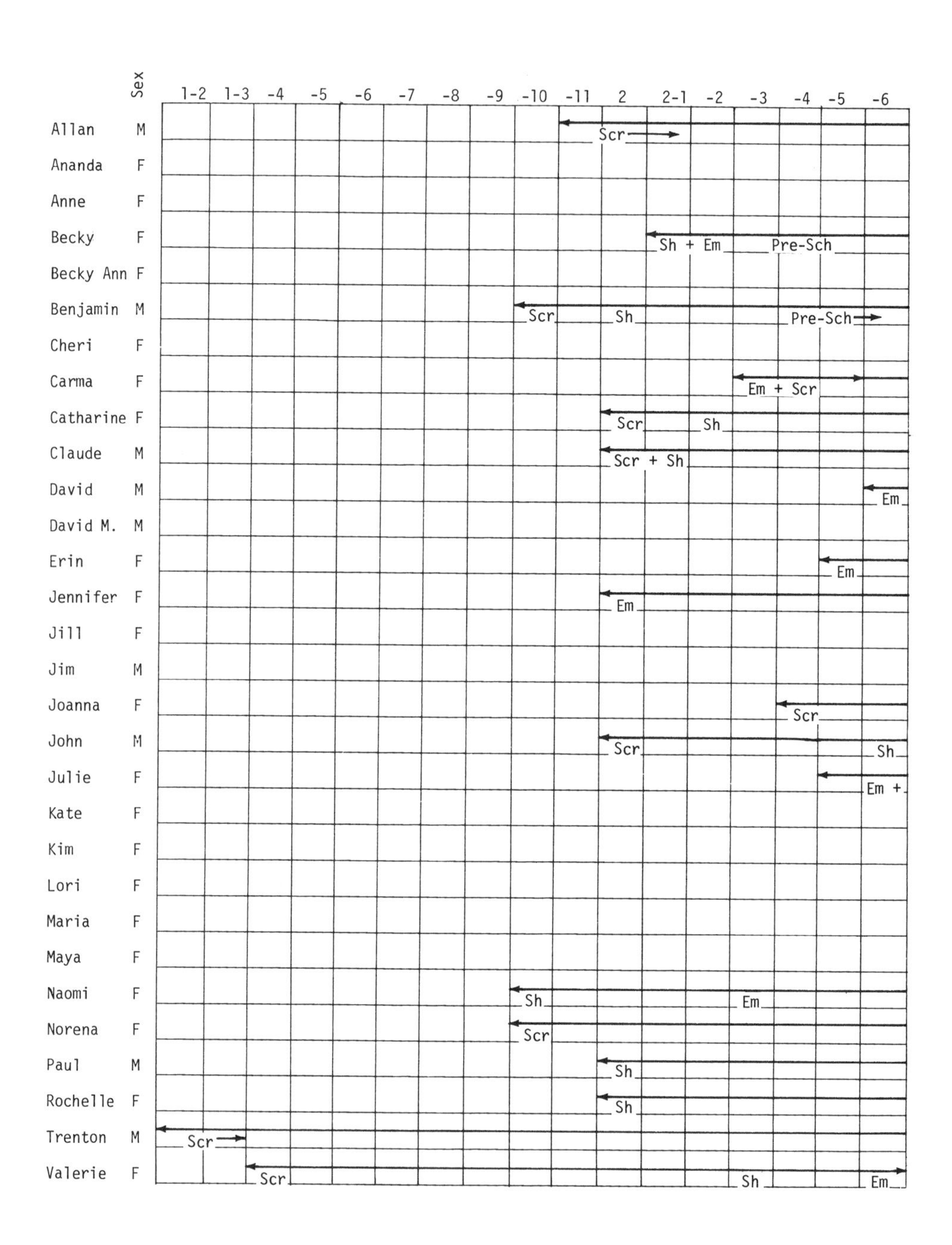

Horizontal numbers — first number = year; second number = additional months as part of year.
⟷ Age range of picture sequence per child.
Scr = Scribble; Sh = Shapes; Em = Emerging figures and objects; Pre-Sch = Preschema; Sch = Schema; dev. Sch = developed Schema; Real = Realism (from nature).
Line = Line drawings mainly; P = Paintings mainly; P+L = both used, neither favored.

-7 -8 -9 -10 -11 3 3¼ -½ -3/4 4 4½ 5 5½ 6 6½ 7 8 9 10 Age

Sequence	Age
Em Pre-Sch	L
Em → Pre-Sch Sch	L
Em + Sh Pre-Sch Sch dev.Sch → + Real →	L+P
+ Scr Sh + Scr Re-Em Pre-Sch + Scr + Sh Sch dev.Sch	L
Sch →	L
Sch dev.Sch	L
dev.Sch + Real + Perspective	L+P
Pre-Sch	L
Em Pre-Sch Sch dev.Sch Real	L+P
Em Pre-Sch Sch → + Real →	L+P
Pre-Sch Sch dev.Sch	L
Em Pre-Sch Sch	L
Pre-Sch dev.Sch dev.Sch	L
Pre-Sch dev.Sch	L
Em Pre-Sch	L
Pre-Sch	L
Sh Em Pre-Sch	P
Em Pre-Sch	L+P
Sh Pre-Sch	L+P
Pre-Sch → Sch → dev.Sch	L(+P)
Sh + Em	P
Em + Sh + Scr Pre-Sch + Sch	P
Sch dev.Sch	L
Em + Scr + Sh + Pre-Sch → Sch	L+P
Pre-Sch → Sch	L
Sh Em	L
Em Pre-Sch	L+P
Em → Pre-Sch Sch	P
Sh Pre-Sch	L+P
Pre-Sch	L

A complete list of all visuals in the program is available in the accompanying *Professional Supplement* (available to instructors). This master list is organized first by child and then in ascending order by age. It provides MEDIAPAK number and frame number, title (in quotes if verbatim by child), age, medium, size (if large or small or tiny), and (for MEDIAPAK 12 only) whether the work was done at school or at home.

Index

Boldface numbers refer to figures.